LIFE LESSONS

A VIEW FROM

THE

HEALING

BED

Gay S. Poe

ISBN 0-9706117-7-3

Design and Production
Riverstone Group, LLC, Canton, GA

Manuscript edited by Carolyn Cunningham

Scripture quotations are from the King James Bible unless noted otherwise.

DEDICATION

I would like to dedicate this book to my precious husband of forty-seven years, Richard, who was called to his heavenly home on November 13, 2000. He had many physical ailments, including heart disease and diabetes. He was always very happy and optimistic about life. He was my most honest critic and my greatest cheerleader. When he passed away, I truly felt I had lost my "better half."

He was active until the very end. He came home on Sunday afternoon after a weekend business trip; and his first words to me were: "Come here. I need a hug." Then he proceeded to tell me how much he loved and appreciated me. I told him how much I loved him; and for all practical purposes, that was our last real conversation. I feel it was God's gift to me.

He had dinner and sat down to read all of his newspapers he had missed while he was away. (He read them in order.) I went into my bedroom to watch TV. My custom was to go in around 1 a.m. and wake him to come to bed. This morning I had fallen asleep and did not wake up until 3 a.m. When I went to wake him, he was sitting in his favorite chair with his hands folded on the paper and his head was leaning against the wing of his chair. When I touched him, I knew he was gone. There was no sign of a struggle – only peace that comes when a Christian sees his Savior for the first time.

There were no hysterics but a peace and gratitude that God had taken him before he had to suffer the ravages of his diabetes that definitely would have followed. After his precious body was taken away, I went to my bedroom and knelt by our bed. I thanked God for giving me such a kind, loving, and optimistic Christian man with whom to share my life and be the father of my children and grandfather to our grandchildren.

For the next two years, I ran. I stayed as busy as I could to keep from facing my loss. I lost fifty pounds, and I wanted to be with him. However, he and I had made a pact that if one of us preceded the other, the one remaining would not die also but would live the rest of their life as fully as possible. The only cure for self-pity is gratitude, and I have so much of that I can hardly contain it. Next year would have been our fiftieth wedding anniversary. It makes me sad; but truly loving him, could I really want to bring his diseased body back from heaven? Gratefully, I know we will meet again in that perfect place God has prepared for us.

FOREWORD

I have been sickly off and on all my life. I had an injury to my neck when I was twelve years old that caused me constant headaches for nearly twenty years. I have had asthma since I was a young child. I am deathly allergic to strong odors – especially perfumes, colognes, and after-shave lotions. Although these different things flared up on occasion, for the most part I could take care of my family and attend college. I earned a degree as a Registered Nurse with much support from my husband, my parents, and many others.

Because my children were young, I did not want to be away from them. I took a position with a large insurance company as a claims processor. This job allowed me to supplement the family income and be home with my family at night. I hated the job and yearned to work with patients again; but looking back, I can see how much GOD taught me by me being there.

In 1971 my headaches began to be unbearable. I went to a neurosurgeon who discovered I had a herniated disc and bone spurs that were causing my head and neck pain. He recommended a cervical fusion. With much fear and trepidation, I gave my consent and he did the surgery and I received immediate relief. It was wonderful! However, my right arm was still weak; and my fingers would get very numb. It was annoying; but compared to the pain, I considered it a bearable inconvenience.

I worked for the insurance company for seven years and could not stand another day of that paperwork. I began working in a hospital because I felt my children were old enough for me to do so.

I loved my nursing and the interactions with the patients. My self-esteem (which had never been too high) was soaring because I felt as if I was making a real contribution to life. Two of my children were teenagers, and my younger son was nine or ten. I was barely twenty and twenty-two when my son and daughter were born. We grew older together. I won't say we grew up because many times I'm not sure any of us has grown up yet. We are still "works in progress."

It was a magical time. I was so happy with my work. All the free time I could spare was spent with my children and their friends who really felt I was the same age as they were because I either instigated or participated in most of their antics. It was one of the most wonderful times of my life, and I treasure it. It still makes me sad to hear parents talk about how bad it is to have teenagers. They don't know what they are missing.

In 1975, after working for a year and a half at my first love, nursing, the symptoms in my right arm began to give me serious problems such as numbness and dropping things, etc. I went back to the neurosurgeon, who had done such a wonderful surgery on my neck, to ask for suggestions. He said he thought the muscle in the right side of my neck was too tight and he could go in and clip it to probably solve my problem.

He explained it was a little "nothing" surgery that could be done on an out-patient basis. However, he said he would feel safer if I spent one night as an inpatient. This time I had no fear at all and had no idea that this little "nothing" surgery would change my whole future.

I was wheeled to surgery at 7 A.M.; and the friend who came with me was told that – even with recovery room time – I would be back in an hour. They finally brought me back to my room at 2:30 P.M., and my friend had almost torn down the hospital because he could not get a straight answer as to where I was and what was going on. I stayed in the hospital for a week – totally drugged out from the Thorazine they kept giving me for the nausea I was experiencing. They never hinted that anything was wrong.

I had the flu right after I returned home, and it was awful. I coughed day and night. When I finally got to my family doctor, he ordered a lung scan. He came in my room and said, "Would you like to tell me where are the other two-thirds of your right lung?" He said, "This is baffling because I have only seen this when the phrenic nerve ,which controls the diaphragm, has been severed." I immediately answered, "Do you mean like this?" – showing him the scar on the right side of my neck. He shook his head and replied, "Exactly like that!"

I was in the hospital for 120 days the first year after it happened and then in for a week or so each month for breathing treatments, cough control, IVs, cortisone, etc. I spent the next three years bedridden with oxygen tanks by my bed.

I passed through all of the stages of grief. I was disbelieving, angry, asking, "Why me?" It has taken many years to reach a place of real acceptance. This acceptance came only after I acknowledged that I have no control over my life, but GOD does. Finally, after a long struggle, I stopped asking "Why?" and asked HIM to use me for whatever HIS plan was for my life. I realize now that I would never have learned TRUE spirituality except by walking the path GOD chose for me. It has been said and is true: "Sometimes GOD has to knock us flat to get us to look up!!"

Because of my experience with chronic health problems and being "housebound" much of the time, GOD has been able to use me to help others deal with health issues. They feel someone with a similar experience is more credible and really understands what they are feeling.

My prayer is that GOD will use some of these writings to help someone in their daily struggles. By going back to my first writings, I can see how far GOD has brought me on this hard, frightening, wonderful journey we call "LIFE."

YOU PLANT THE SEEDS!

Are you ever afraid
Of what you have to do –
Even though you're convinced
It's what GOD wants from you?

Our hearts filled with terror
With our imperfections,
We feel so unworthy –
We don't like rejections.

We wish that these urges
Would leave us in peace;
But with each passing day,
Pressures increase.

HOLY HINTS from above,
Like snowflakes, keep falling
To make sure we know
Exactly Who's calling!

Go ahead. Use me, LORD,
In spite of my fear.
Just promise YOUR VOICE
Will always be clear.

So hold my hand please.
Wrap my fear in YOUR LOVE.
I'll be trusting directions
You send from above.

I claim YOUR PROMISE.
YOU will give what I need.
I will make the words blossom
If YOU plant the seed!

INTRODUCTION

*U*nashamedly, I confess I have always been reluctant to put my writing in a form that could be presented to the public. Fear of rejection (in the guise of being too busy, not feeling well, or having too many other commitments) was the real culprit that made me keep it in an old briefcase in the closet. I, like most, do not handle rejection well.

My husband always encouraged me. He would say, "On any occasion when you've read something that you've written, I have never seen anything but people crying, laughing, or touched in an emotional manner. You have a God-given gift, and you should be ashamed to hide it in the closet."

I realize now that writing is how I talk to God and also how HE speaks to me. I became aware of this when we were packing for a trip and I wanted to take my writings with me. I knew, if they were lost or destroyed, I could never recreate them. Truly, I can remember the NAMES of only a few poems – much less the WORDS! I think God lets me forget so that when I reread them I get a new message from HIM and I learn each time.

A few years ago, God saw fit to place a person in my life who is even more stubborn than I am. He challenged me to a wager: "You read a poem to the group you are attending tonight. If you don't receive any positive reinforcement, then we'll forget it and I'll never mention it again. If you do, however, you will make the effort." I agreed.

I shared a poem from this book with the group, and the response was very positive; but I was still paralyzed by my fear and did nothing. My friend never mentioned it again, but he and I both knew I had "welched" on our bargain.

One Sunday morning as I watched a church service on TV, the minister said, "Do you know who I really feel sorry for?" I was expecting most anything except what I heard that hit me like a "body blow." He said, "It is someone God has given something to do for HIM, and they keep refusing to do it!" It seemed he was looking straight at me, and God's message was clear: "JUST START!! LEAVE THE RESULTS TO ME!!!"

With this effort, I am stepping out in faith to do my ten percent – that is, my footwork – and trust God to take care of the other ninety percent. With this new attitude, the pressure and fear are taken from me and put in "GOD'S HANDS" where they have always belonged. God will do for me what I cannot do for myself if I get out of my own way and let HIM take care of things.

I compare it with a two year old trying to tie his shoes. He doesn't know how, but he keeps pushing help away until he is weary and thoroughly frustrated. I have struggled for so long, endeavoring to do it myself and it simply doesn't work. Armed with the promise that God is ready and willing to help if I just give up the struggle, I want to "LET GO AND LET GOD"!

The words of the preceding poem describe the bargain I made with MYSELF (God doesn't make bargains). I'll write HIS WORDS if "HE PLANTS THE SEEDS"!!! MAYFLOWER or TITANIC – it's GOD'S decision; and either way, I'm off the hook!

W H Y ?

Why? We ask when the going gets rough
And life seems hopeless and long.
Why? We ask when pain racks our soul
And living seems useless and wrong.

Where is this GOD, full of mercy and love,
Who we've learned about since a child?
Why should we suffer when we try to be good
While others are wicked and wild?

Do we ever ask "WHY" when the way is smooth
And the world is singing our song?
Do we think about GOD when life's going well
And everyone is healthy and strong?

No! We take it for granted and forget to say "thanks"
And suppose all these blessings are due us.
When we look at our lives, only mercy and love
Can explain GOD'S Goodness to us!

So stop, precious child, and consider your life
And the blessings GOD has allowed you.
You will see very soon that they outweigh the bad
And with purpose GOD has endowed you.

Don't gripe and complain 'bout your plight in life.
Just relax and let GOD guide you.
HIS TIMETABLE isn't ever like yours,
But HE promises HE is beside you.

GOD knows when we stumble and fall on our way.
HE knows when our heart is breaking.
Just trust HIM, for HE can see all of the path.
HE knows every step we'll be taking.

So do not waste your energy wondering "WHY"
When it seems GOD'S not doing HIS part.
He'll make your life whole and accomplish HIS GOAL
If you trust HIM with all of your heart.

DO YOU REALLY TRUST ME?

*A*s human beings, we are inclined to base our attitudes, actions, and moods on how we happen to be feeling on that particular day. Webster's Dictionary describes FEELING as any subjective reaction – either pleasurable or unpleasurable – that one may have to a situation and usually connotes an absence of reason. Therefore, if our beliefs, actions, attitudes, etc. were based entirely on our feelings, there would be no reality in our lives. Many times we are called upon to do things we don't FEEL like doing just because they are the right things to do – no matter how we may feel.

Sometimes our faith falters due to negative feelings. Faith is based on reality and should never, therefore, depend on feelings that swing back and forth from day to day or even hour to hour.

If we really trust God, we will have an inner peace that will sustain us and assure us that God is in charge and everything will be okay – no matter what cards life deals us or how we might feel each day. It is easy to give lip service to our trust in God but only as we live and practice this trust in our lives do we answer the question:

DO YOU REALLY TRUST ME?

You may say that you trust Me. Then please tell Me why
You sit and you worry 'bout who'll live and who'll die?

Is it only when life's smooth that your faith is strong,
Or does it falter and weaken when things seem to go wrong?

It takes no real hero to trust without fear
When your world is secure and no danger seems near.

It's when there is trouble, more problems than joys,
That real faith separates the men from the boys.

With our mouths we can preach from morning 'til night
How IN GOD WE TRUST and He'll do what is right;

But our actions speak louder than our words ever do,
And the people around can see what is true.

God loves us all, and HE had a plan
To make the most of each life if we'll take His hand.

So if He holds the future of each person we know,
Why is it so hard just letting things go?

So pray that 'ole prayer that's been put to the test—
To change what we can and accept all the rest.

And remember, dear friend, as you frettingly plod,
When you're frightened and worried, you're insulting God!!!

THE HEALING BED

*M*any people who know me – and all those who do not – are probably wondering why I chose this title for this book. Believe me, it was not a spur-of-the-moment decision. I ran many titles through my mental processor; but after much reflection, I realized the most important lessons and insights I have learned were during times of pain and pleasure that came to me while I was chained to that old bed of ours.

It is interesting in rearing a family that the moments which are burned into your memory as frightening and painful sometimes turn out to be the most precious. My husband and I had a king-sized bed. It was always large enough that if one of our children was sick or afraid from a bad dream, they knew there was always room between Mom and Pop for them to feel safe and warm and secure. They are now forty-five, forty-three, and thirty-five, respectively; and they still feel that way. My daughter was always pretty independent, so she did not indulge as much – except in her teenage years.

Last Christmas, my oldest son was diagnosed with pneumonia after a bout with the flu; while my younger son was having a problem with an abscessed tooth. The younger, who is unmarried, had come home for Christmas and had to go straight to the dentist. Immediately thereafter, he was in the "healing bed," under my electric blanket, watching TV. I am sure if my older son could have had his choice, he would have been there too. There is still some "magic" in that old bed that makes them feel safe. They always know their "mom" is near.

My older son still feels the "healing bed" – as it is affectionately called – is the only place he can get well. One of the reasons I love my daughter-in-law Pris so much is because a few months after they were married my son got sick and came by my house after seeing the doctor. She called while he was still here – knowing he would be in our bed – and said, "Dave, if you will feel better in your mom and dad's bed, you can stay there. I won't mind." I did not leave the decision to him but told him – in no uncertain terms – that he was a grown man and her husband and his place was with her in their bed. The mother in me wanted him to stay, but the wife in me knew it was a mistake.

Because of all my health problems, I spend a lot of time in that bed still; but at one point in my life, I spent three solid years in it. It became a meeting place for both my children and their friends. This is where they came to share their funny stories, successes, failures, romances, and all the important events in their lives.

When my children are hurting – either physically or mentally, they still migrate to that old bed; and we share feelings, disappointments, heartaches, and joys. The joy far outweighs the disappointments. Just as my children learned by unconditional love and care, so did I. GOD used this bed to teach me many lessons about how much HE loves me. HE taught me that HIS LOVE, HIS UNDERSTANDING, and HIS UNFAILING EVERLAST-ING ARMS were there to carry me through my pain or hurt I was enduring – if I gave up the struggle and asked for HIS HELP. I learned spirituality and how to pray in that bed.

The "HEALING BED" and the special happiness it has provided me – as well as the lessons I have learned there – are a GOD-GIVEN GIFT! When I was thirty-five and a prisoner in that bed, I spent many hours alone. We are in the catering and concession business, and my family worked long hours which meant I was alone a great deal of the time. You can only watch so much TV, read so many books, and make so many phone calls before you must stop running and realize GOD wants to tell you something and you SHOULD lis-ten. When I finally listened, my struggles, fear, loneliness, and self-pity were replaced by peace, serenity, gratitude, and contentment. GOD did for me what I could not do for myself – but only when I asked HIM.

HOW DO YOU SAY 'GOODBYE'?

I would like to tell you about the first man I ever met. He was a distinguished man with fringes of hair around the edge of his beautiful bald head. I don't remember much about our first meeting because I was very young. As a matter of fact, he was the first man to hold me in his arms. I can't recall, but I am sure I felt very safe because he always had that effect on me. I knew I could always depend on him and that he would be there for me, and he was until the day he died.

As you may have guessed by now, it was Dr. John C. Holley, Sr. who delivered me – as well as most of the kids of my generation. I was very grateful that my parents ignored his suggestion that I be named "Saphronia"; but other than that, I could never find much fault with him.

Dr. Holley used to call my "Grandma Jernigan" (who died when I was only two) to go with him to make house calls and care for people when he had a particularly difficult situation. She had no formal training, but she was a born nurse and loved helping sick people. When I received my nursing degree, he was the first one to whom I wanted to show my nursing pin. I remember vividly what he said, "If you turn out to be half the nurse your grandma was, you will be just fine."

We lived in a small town where everyone knew everyone else and we all took care of each other. We ran to Dr. Holley with any little ailment – from sore throats to broken arms, and he always made things better. There were five of us in my immediate family, and we went to him on an average of at least once a week. He only billed my dad once a year; and one year the bill was $35 (that included my brother's broken arm, sutures, and God only knows what else). I do recall, however, that my daddy always took him fresh fish when he caught any.

It reminds me of "Little House on the Prairie" because back then Dr. Holley did the unthinkable: he made house calls! I doubt the $35 my dad paid him took care of his gasoline and car repairs. Dr. Holley drove a blue Buick, and I always felt better when I saw his car coming (except when I was sick because of something I did that he had told me not to do). He expected his orders to be obeyed without question.

Once, when I was about fifteen, I had a bad case of bronchitis; and my mom made me go see him. He examined me, gave me a prescription, and told me to go home and go straight to bed. My part-time job was cutting a stencil and running the church bulletin. It was the day it was to be done, so I decided to do it before I went home to bed. As luck would have it, Dr. Holley drove by the church and saw me. He shook his finger at me, and he had already called my mom at work to tell her what I did before I even got home.

After I was married and had two children, we moved back to Milton and my whole family went to him for each "sniffle" — just the same as when we were kids. Each time I would walk to "Mrs. Winnie Campbell's" desk to pay the bill, the chart would say: "No charge." After this happened a few times, I went back in his office to protest; and he said, "Don't worry about it. I'll put it on your daddy's bill." Of course, he never did.

He was truly like family. He was very young when he first came to Milton to practice. When my mom and Aunt Glennis, who was only six years old, contracted typhoid fever, he treated them. He had had typhoid when he was young. As a result his hair came out and never came back. My mom was very sick and lost all her hair and had to learn to walk all over again. One of the first advocates of "women's rights," my Aunt Glennis wanted her hair to fall out, so she could look like Dr. Holley.

Dr. Holley's wife, Lucille, was my piano teacher. She would get very frustrated when she thought I hadn't practiced (I probably had not) and would bang my fingers on the piano. Occasionally, Dr. Holley would come home unexpectedly in the afternoon; and her method of teaching would change drastically. Apparently, he would get after her if he thought she was picking on me. Needless to say, I was always happy to hear his car drive up.

I was devastated when he suffered for a long time and finally died with lung cancer. I saw him a few days before he died; and as sick as he was, he still managed to scold me about my weight. That was my last visit with him, and

I still miss him. He was truly special, and I loved him very much!

He was the typical country doctor by today's standards, but he was a fantastic diagnostician. More than all that, he had a special quality that is so rare: he CARED. He was always available to those who needed him DAY or NIGHT.

His son, Dr. John C. Holley, Jr. delivered my last child. He told me his dad coached him all through my pregnancy because he wanted to be sure "his girl" received the proper care.

God picked a rare prize when he took our Dr. Holley. Everyone in Milton, Florida missed him. I still do!

HOW DO YOU SAY 'GOODBYE'?

How do you say "goodbye" to a friend
Whom you've known and loved for so long?
What fills the void of his precious face
And his words that made you feel strong?

What takes the place of his loving touch
When fear is wrenching your soul –
The reassurance only he could give
That made you cheer up and be bold?

Do you ever stop missing that special voice
With the lilt that could make your whole day?
Do you ever learn to go it alone
And cope in some other way?

You DON'T say "goodbye" to such a friend.
You just weep and let GOD comfort you.
You thank the LORD for the time you had
And that love from this friendship grew.

Thank You, LORD, for this wonderful friend
With whose life mine so intertwined.
I'm grateful that I could be part of his life
As he was a BIG part of mine.

I CANNOT CHANGE THE WIND

*O*ne of my favorite stories in the Bible is the one when the great storm with the strong winds and high waves came up suddenly on the Sea of Galilee. JESUS and His disciples were on board.

As it is related in the Bible, they left the shore and there was only a gentle breeze and the water was calm and smooth as glass. JESUS was weary from talking with and healing people all day; so He went down into the boat to rest, and HE fell asleep.

While JESUS slept, the winds whipped up and the waves were beginning to wash over the small boat. His disciples became very afraid and were certain they would die.

Excitedly, they woke JESUS who had many times before questioned their faith. Immediately, He calmed the winds and the waves. One of the disciples asked, "Who is this man that even the winds and the waves obey Him?"

As I progress on my spiritual journey, I become more and more aware of who this Man was and even more importantly who HE is. There is a popular song with lyrics that suggests you: "Put your hand in the hand of the MAN who stilled the water."

Every day now I strive to do this. I now realize that even though I cannot "change the winds" – if I trust MY FATHER enough, HE will give me the willingness and courage to "adjust the sails" to go in the direction HE is leading.

I CANNOT CHANGE THE WIND

Father and son
Set out one day,
And the sun was bright
As they sailed away.

They fished and played
And had such fun.
The father was proud
Of his fine, young son.

The boy thought his father
Was strong and brave
As he captained the boat
Over every wave.

As they enjoyed
Their fun, little lark,
They began to notice
That the sky was dark.

The wind was strong
And the waves got high
And the scared, little boy
Thought they both might die!

The father seemed calm
And in control.
He knew what to do
As his son he told,

"I cannot change the wind."
His frightened, young son paled.
"But GOD will always show me
How I must adjust the sail."

MAMIE

"*M*amie" is self-explanatory. She was the black lady who cared for my brothers and me when we were small. My mother had to work to help my dad keep us fed and clothed.

She loved us very much and especially me. I was just a toddler and the only girl. I gave her "unconditional" love.

She called me her "baby" from the first day she came to our home until the last time I saw her just a few weeks before her death. She was very ill and almost blind from her diabetes; but she still recognized her baby's voice and touch, and I could still feel her love in her hug.

The last time I visited her, I read her this poem and she wanted it read at her funeral. Once again, GOD gave me the gift of being able to tell someone how much I loved him or her before it was too late.

'MAMIE'

I was born in '35,
And things were kind of tough.
Both Mom and Daddy had to work.
Things were pretty rough.

A lady came and cooked and cleaned
And cared for all us kids.
She called us all her "babies."
There was love in all she did.

She'd let me help make biscuits.
I always did it wrong,
But she praised my work and built my pride –
Though it took her twice as long.

She'd comb the "rats and witches"
Out of my tangled hair,
And it seemed each time we needed her
That she was always there.

She would rock me in her lap
'Til that "Sandman" he would win,
And she'd sing how "Jesus Loves Me" –
How He'd always be my Friend.

With her rolled stockings on my feet,
I'd stomp in her old shoes.
I'd get by with anything.
I knew I'd never lose.

Her "baby" – as she called me –
Never understood the fact
That even when I scrubbed her face,
It always would stay black.

Time has past, and she is old.
My babies are all grown,
But memories of her love for me
Have a way of hanging on.

Her health is bad; her sight is dimmed;
But in our mind's eye, we both see
That young black woman and a little white girl
That just happened to be her and me.

She preceded me to Heaven,
And I know she'll sit and wait
To say, "Here comes my baby,
LORD. Open up that gate!"

FREEDOM

I remember the Fourth of July as a fun and happy day sparked with the anticipation of family gatherings, good food, and the promise of fireworks to light up the hot and humid Florida nighttime. We had a place where we always met family and friends called FLORIDA TOWN on the bay – almost midpoint between Milton and Pensacola, Florida. There was not a lot to recommend it except the large, old oak trees strung with streamers of Spanish moss.

There was an old hotel that was built during the Florida Boom in the 1920s and boasted the first inground swimming pool I had ever seen. During the boom, many such elegant hotels sprang up and just as suddenly became vacant and fell into disrepair after the stock market crash in 1929.

I loved these old fantasy buildings that had been so modern for that day and age. I can remember as a child of six or seven wandering through one such abandoned hotel, being enchanted by the fact that there was a telephone in every room. They were like "sleeping giants" that had been cut down in their prime. These places made me very sad. However, I never thought of Florida Town as a sad place because it held so many wonderful memories for me.

My immediate family and my extended family (aunts, uncles, and cousins, etc.) used to all meet here at the halfway point. We would spread blankets under the shade of those large oak trees, and soon the blankets were covered with all our favorite foods.

Each aunt brought her specialty – from southern fried chicken to mouth-watering potato salad. There were unbelievable desserts, including homemade ice cream, pies, cakes, and the all-American favorite, watermelon.

All the children played games, and we delighted ourselves in ways children in the present generation would not even understand. Exactly one hour after lunch (that was the rule), we would all go swimming and have the time of our lives.

The adults fanned and gossiped, while we enjoyed the refreshingly cool water.

Later in the afternoon, we would eat again, swim again; and just before it got too dark to see, we would get out the fireworks (there were no gigantic firework displays like those available to us now). We were both awed and delighted by such simple things as sparklers, Chinese firecrackers, and bottle rockets. Although we were warned repeatedly about the danger of fireworks, I remember my older brother lighting a firecracker and not tossing it quickly enough. It exploded in his hand, and he was burned rather badly.

As the population of our town grew with the installation of Whiting Field Naval Air Training Station, INDEPENDENCE DAY and its celebration took on a larger flavor. There would be a parade with the naval drill team performing, while the high school band (of which I was a member) would be playing a variety of Sousa marches. Open convertibles with beauty queen contestants adorning the back seats would pass by. They would wave and throw candy, and we thought we were really great if we managed to retrieve a piece or two.

The local fire truck (yes, just one); the ambulance; and any classic cars or horses anyone might own would take part. My favorite part was when the honor guard would march by so straight and tall. As they marched past in such a straight line with our AMERICAN FLAG waving proudly in the summer breeze (if we were fortunate enough to have a breeze that time of year), I could never hold back the tears of pride.

I cannot remember a time upon seeing an American flag waving that I did not have a thrill of pride and excitement wash over me. Even before I had ever been to school and taught what freedom, independence, and the flag meant, I had an instinctive feeling (perhaps derived from my parents and family) that made me know this flag and the freedom it represented were a special blessing that was not enjoyed by everyone. It should be revered and cherished.

As I have grown older, I am ashamed to admit that this wonderful gift – for which so many brave men and women have died – has been taken for granted. When I see the nightly news and the suffering many people are going through – with no voice or means of escape for them or their children, my heart goes out to them. However, I cannot internalize this feeling and truly appreciate that my parents, my husband and I, my children, or my grandchildren have not had to suffer the terrible atrocities of those who have no freedom.

I am heartsick that many of us have forgotten why we fought the Revolution and won our independence in 1776. We were fighting tyranny, and we were willing to die for what we believed. Now we are so apathetic that the only dealings many have politically are to complain about whoever is in office and what they are doing.

Part of our freedom is freedom of worship. That is the reason the Pilgrims came to this country. They were fighting for the right to worship as they chose, and GOD blessed them. Recently, it seems, some in power are fighting just as hard to tear down that religious freedom that so many suffered to win. There are those who would choose to strip away all semblances of religion and the GOD who has blessed us for more than two hundred years.

Year after year, Fourth of July celebrations get larger and more elaborate. Is this progress? It definitely IS NOT if we get so caught up in the hype that we forget who will be and has always been responsible for our good fortune.

BROTHER JOE

*W*hen I was twelve years old, I met the new pastor of our church. Little did I know what an impact this wonderful man would have on my life. He became – and still is – one of my dearest and most trusted friends. He has been a part of almost every important and meaningful event that has taken place in my life. God's love shone in his eyes, and there was never any doubt that he and GOD were involved in an intimate relationship.

Unfortunately, there are some people who feel that spirituality and fun are incompatible; but this man was living proof that they complemented each other. We always knew he was available for serious counseling, but we also knew he was always ready to participate in our fun times. Many times he was the RING leader!

He drew people of all ages to him like a magnet because of his wit and charm but mostly because we could feel his closeness to GOD. We wanted what he had!

For fifty-two years, I have loved and respected "Brother Joe." This little love note tells him how I feel.

BROTHER JOE

There's a man in our town I'm sure that you know.
He's affectionately known as Ole Brother Joe!

Seems I've always known him in joy or in strife.
He has always shared the events in my life.

He called us "his kids"; now we are all grown.
Now it seems all "his kids" have kids of their own.

He made us laugh and gave us such a thrill,
Tickling the ivories to "'Ole Steamboat Bill"!!

He would speak at our school; we'd be so proud.
The children all loved him; he enchanted the crowd.

"Preachers are dull!" other church kids would say.
"But Brother Joe's different in a fun sort of way."

He was jolly and fun, but he also was firm.
If we did something wrong, a look made us squirm!

Sometimes we would falter, and we'd go astray;
But he'd pray and he'd love us back to the way.

When I grew up, he changed my whole life
When he said the words, "You're now man and wife."

When my babies were born, he started again.
He repeated the cycle as he made them a friend.

In sickness, his prayers made me know I'd be fine.
I feel he's so special; he has a "hot line."

When loved ones have died and the heart's full of grief,
His words of comfort always brought great relief!

He fought for right when wrong seemed the best.
He set an example; could we dare to do less?

When the PEARLY GATES open, one reason will be
Because of the influence his life had on me.

A voice I will hear; it will happen I know:
"Here comes another. WELL DONE! BROTHER JOE."

ELLA LEE

*M*iss Ella Lee Cobb was a classmate of my mom's all during their high school years. Ella Lee was an exceptionally intelligent and devout Christian young lady. She had a great sense of humor, and everyone who knew her loved her.

It had always been Miss Ella Lee's plan to be a missionary to China when she graduated from college. She had done everything necessary to fulfill this plan.

Just as it was almost time for her to sail, she was afflicted with some strange malady. I am not certain that even today they are sure what her problem was (probably some muscular or neurological degeneration). She got weaker and weaker. Finally, she became totally bedridden. The people in our small hometown could not imagine how this could happen.

Only GOD and ELLA LEE know what feelings of frustration, disappointment, anger, denial, and grief she probably experienced; but she worked through it with the sweetest spirit of almost anyone I have ever known. She trusted GOD that HE had a different and better plan for her.

For sixty years, she was bedridden. People would go to see her at first out of a feeling of pity and duty; but after awhile, they began to realize that a visit with Ella Lee was not a depressing duty to be endured but a blessing and a privilege. She was always so radiant and happy; YOU were the one cheered up after the visit. She spent her time alone making phone calls to shut-ins and sending birthday cards, sympathy cards, or just a note of encouragement that always came just when you needed it most.

The only time she had the opportunity to leave her home was when she was taken by ambulance for some medical procedure. As a special treat at Christmas, some of the local ambulance services would drive her around town to see the Christmas lights and decorations.

She was more of a missionary from her bed and touched more lives with her sweet, loving spirit than she could possibly have touched by going to China. She was a legend in that community – a testimony to how circumstances that seem senseless benefit so many.

'ELLA LEE — GOD'S WAY'

My mom had a friend;
They were classmates for years.
They shared lots of laughter
And a few silly tears.

This lady was special —
Her face always aglow
Because after graduation
She planned to go

To a faraway land —
Anywhere that GOD led,
To be HIS MISSIONARY,
HIS WORD to help spread.

As it came time to sail,
Her plans had to change —
Completely bedridden,
Her life rearranged.

All those who knew of her
And her lofty plan
Were bewildered and puzzled,
But she trusted GOD'S plan.

For sixty long years,
She still did not know;
But her FAITH never wavered.
Her sweet, frail face kept its glow.

She was in pain;
She tried hard not to show it.
With one look at that frail, little body,
You'd know it.

Life takes strange turns —
Quality to increase.
GOD sees the whole picture;
We see only a piece.

GOD, use me like this one —
To accept and obey.
Give me strength and patience
To do things YOUR BETTER WAY!

HAPPY TRAILS TO YOU

*R*ecently, I had an occasion to buy a Christmas gift for a friend of mine. Like me, he is well over twenty-one; and sometimes we get together and reminisce about the things we remember about our childhood and some of the heroes we had in common in our younger years.

As I shopped, I tried to think of something nostalgic that would make him wander back to those younger years when we were not beset on every hand by the pressures with which the children of today must deal. Many times we had talked about the Saturday movies we used to enjoy. Now we pay $6.75 to attend a movie and see several previews of coming attractions and commercials, describing all of the delicious candy, popcorn, soft drinks, etc. that can be bought in the lobby. Hopefully, you can pay for it with your child's college fund. Then we see the feature presentation, and the whole experience takes about two hours.

When we were kids, we could go to the movies for fifteen cents and stay all day. There would be a couple of features (always westerns), several cartoons, and a serial – like Captain Midnight or Buck Rogers or some other superhero. Always at the end of the serial, the hero would be hanging from a cliff or be tied to the train tracks with the train fast approaching or going over a waterfall or (my personal favorite) be tied to the lumber mill conveyor belt with a rapidly approaching "buzz saw." The only outcome could be impending doom; and it made us all want to do chores, save bottle caps, or whatever it took to get the fifteen cents to see what happened next week. It didn't take us long to figure out that every week the hero would be left in dire straits, so we would be "hooked" and absolutely have to be there the next Saturday.

"Anybody" who was "anybody" was at the movies on Saturday morning. Unlike nowadays, the movie did not stop after each showing. It ran continuously. For our fifteen cents, we were allowed to watch it over and over.

My brother, who is five and a half years older than I am, was the part-time projectionist at the theater. He used to kid me by saying, "My job on Saturday night is sweeping out all the DEAD COWBOYS!"

The Saturday movie was a social event where we all met; and if we were lucky, our lunch consisted of popcorn, candy bars, and sodas. It was wonderful!

During this time, we could forget all our troubles and completely immerse ourselves in the predictable plots that were offered for our enjoyment. There were so many heroes who galloped across the Silver Screen that it was hard to decide who were our favorites. Roy Rogers, Gene Autry, The Cisco Kid, Tim Holt, and "Lash" Larue are a few who come to mind.

Our home was directly behind the only theater in town. One of my most exciting memories was sitting in the swing on our front porch, watching "Lash" practicing with his whip for the stage show he would be putting on that evening. He smiled at me and said "Hi," and I thought I would die from sheer excitement. After all, I was a ten-year-old girl; and he was the great "Lash." (I could call him that now because, as far as I was concerned, we had met and we were FRIENDS!!) No one has an imagination like a "smitten" ten-year-old girl.

Even though I loved Gene Autry and his horse "Champion" and The Lone Ranger and his horse "Silver" and many other western heroes, NONE could compare with Roy Rogers (THE KING OF THE COWBOYS)! He was really the best and definitely my personal favorite. I spoke of him with the same respect my dad used when he spoke of WILLIAM S. HART, the hottest cowboy of his era. William was on the silent screen, so all he had were subtitles to let people know his thoughts and genius.

Roy's first love was "Trigger" (his golden Palomino). That horse could do everything – from pulling Roy out of tight spots to going for help if he couldn't handle the situation himself. Trigger was so loved that when he died he was stuffed and mounted on his hind legs and has a prominent place in the Roy Rogers Museum.

Roy's comic relief was "Gabby Hayes" (the toothless, old sidekick who was always ready at a moment's notice to assist Roy in his feats of bravery.) Roy was a singing cowboy; and wherever he was – when it was time for him to sing a song, "Bob Nolan and the Sons of the Pioneers" – as well as Roy's guitar – were always on hand for backup. Later on, Dale Evans, Roy's wife who became known as "THE QUEEN OF THE WEST," was included in the ensemble.

The plots of these old westerns – no matter what superhero was involved – were all about the same with little variations – in a feeble attempt to surprise their young viewers (their target audience). A group of bad guys would try to start trouble by taking over the town, stealing some poor rancher's cattle, land, or water rights. The hero would come in, and there would be a gunfight and a fistfight; and the hero would figure out a way to save the girl, the town, and the day – in that order. He would kiss his horse (never the girl), and he would ride into the sunset to await another situation that needed his hero expertise.

There is a lot to be said about the simplicity of these films and the lessons they taught young people. Right and truth always won out. Cheating, lying, and stealing were never rewarded; and we went home feeling good about life, our heroes, and ourselves.

Our problems today come from the fact that young people have so few heroes. Now because of the speed and depth of TV coverage, it seems that most of today's heroes (like movie stars, athletes, and yes, even those who profess to be Christians) are self-centered and only care about what they want and how to get it – no matter what the consequences. Sex and violence keep children afraid, and the false advertising on TV keep them from feeling good about themselves.

I am sure that kids nowadays would think our heroes were pretty "hokey" and boring and would not sit through a whole movie. To me, it is very comforting as I look back. Roy never had to worry about Gene Autry sneaking around and having an affair with Dale Evans. It was a simpler time, and it was great to know that justice would prevail because that was right. We could easily identify the "Villains with their BLACK HATS" from the "Heroes in their WHITE HATS"!

By the way, I received my first kiss from a first-grade classmate on a Saturday morning long ago at a western movie. It was wonderful and exciting, and nobody even considered charging him with "sexual harassment"!!!

IN THE TWINKLING OF GOD'S EYE

*T*he sleepy, little town in northwest Florida where I grew up had majestic oak trees covered with Spanish moss; drugstore sodas; unlocked doors; friendly waves; streets you were not afraid to walk along at night; and a movie theater where for fifteen cents you could spend a whole Saturday with Roy Rogers, Gene Autry, and Captain Midnight. However, it is no more. Compared to the years when I was growing up, it is now a "thriving metropolis." The kids there now have McDonald's, Wendy's, Hardee's, Kentucky Fried Chicken, and all the other well-known chains. They also have various and sundry restaurants all over town.

When I was a teenager, we had a couple of restaurants, one theater, and the "Palms drive-in" where we all hung out. Now there are more banks, churches, doctors, lawyers, supermarkets, schools, etc.; and the population has more than quadrupled since this simple, little town was my "natural habitat."

Back then, everyone knew everyone. All the adults kept an eye on each other's children. The family doctor and your church pastor knew all about you – both physically and morally; and they cared enough to check up on you and pray for you to see that these areas of your life were intact. Sometimes we could slip something by them – but not often!

There were five of us girls who did everything together. We were affectionately known by the townfolks as the "BIG FIVE." We all had our steady beaus. I had gone steady with mine for five years. Everyone in town assumed that one day – when we both had finished high school – he and I would be married. So did we.

Little did I know this was to be my first real experience in learning that OUR plans are just that – OUR plans. We both attended church regularly and were Christians, and we always asked that GOD'S WILL be done in our lives. It also was to be my first experience with this advice: "Be careful what you pray for because you might get it."

Gradually, things began to change between us. His family moved to another town about twenty-five miles away, so we did not see each other as much. We did not have our own automobiles as most kids do now. I began to have the sinking feeling that something was wrong. It seemed when I tried to pray that my boyfriend's face was a block between GOD and me.

When we talked, we both agreed that we did not know what was wrong but we knew something was not right. During this time, he met someone in the church he attended in his new hometown.

One day he came to the school and called me out of band practice and begged me to go to Mississippi (no waiting for blood tests) and get married. Thank GOD I was given the good sense to know if something had to be done that quickly it was most likely a mistake.

I said, "NO." He went home, became engaged to the other girl, and was soon married. I was totally confused and devastated. The sense of abandonment was almost unbearable. I wondered why GOD would allow me to suffer such pain.

I dated some in my senior year, but I wasn't really happy. Graduation came, and it was time for me to go to college and venture into a world where I would be virtually on my own. It was the first time I had ever been away from home. Since the college was several hundred miles from home, my first visit back was not for six long weeks. One of the "BIG FIVE" was my college roommate; but even together, we were MAJOR HOMESICK! She was engaged to her high school sweetheart back home so that curtailed most of her social life.

One day as I sat alone in the college bookstore (which happened to be almost completely empty because it was 3 p.m.), a spindly young man walked up with the "corniest" line I had ever heard. He said, "May I sit with you? (he was a senior majoring in English) It is awfully crowded in here." I was so amused at him having the nerve to say such a thing that I said, "Sure!" We talked for about an hour. Then he asked me to lunch for the following day; and I said, "Yes."

By the next day, I was getting cold feet and did not want to keep the date; but my housemother, who knew my situation, insisted that I go; so I did. I enjoyed his company and was asked out for the next night which was Friday, again on Saturday, and again on Sunday when he gave me a diamond engagement ring. I don't know what surprised me more – his giving it to me or me accepting it. I had only been at college ten days. I can't imagine why (except GOD'S PEACE), but I was not worried and had no reservations because it felt right.

He gave me the ring on September 25; but I told him I could not wear it until I went home and told my parents, and he agreed. We went out every night; and each time we went out, I was more sure that this was GOD'S plan. Back then, curfew for freshman girls was 9:30 p.m. Every night I got back to the dorm at 9:29 p.m., and my roommate would be walking the floor on the front porch waiting for me. She was a "basket case" that whole year.

I went home on October 16 to be in a friend's wedding – with my engagement ring packed carefully away in my luggage. I told my folks; and to say they were shocked was the understatement of the century, but they adjusted. I put on my beautiful ring and called my fiancee long distance to tell him we were officially engaged.

When I went to my friend's wedding, one of the first people I saw was my old beau. He is a sweet man, and I'll always treasure those happy and sometimes unhappy high school years we shared; but I knew GOD'S PLAN was much better than mine, and I felt blessed.

My husband and I were married on June 9. We are the only couple on record – before or since – that caused Wednesday evening prayer meeting to have a time change, so we could be married at 8 p.m. It was my mom and dad's twenty-sixth wedding anniversary, and we wanted to share it since they had done so well.

Since that warm June night with four hundred or so friends to wish us well, we have shared much laughter and many tears. We have been blessed with three wonderful children and four exceptional grandchildren and a great-granddaughter that is too smart and beautiful to describe (I am not prejudiced at all). Financially, we are not wealthy; but we are comfortable and very rich in the blessings that really matter. My husband is a kind, Christian gentleman who gives unselfishly to us all. I can remember very few days that he has not given me a hug and told me how much he loves and appreciates me.

I am truly blessed! June 9 of this year we will celebrate our forty-sixth anniversary. We have outlived most of the skeptics that were sure it would not last because it happened so quickly. What I knew – that they did not – was that our marriage was GOD'S PLAN, not ours; and HE can accomplish HIS PLAN in "the Twinkling of the Eye."

There are many events in my life that I have questioned and wondered if I did the right thing, but my marriage was never one of them. I know I have spent my life with the man GOD chose for me. Thank You, DEAR LORD, for giving me what I NEED which is not usually at all what I think I WANT!

By the way, my old beau and his wife have been happily married as long as we have. GOD did the same thing for him that HE did for me.

MY RICH

*S*ome of my friends seem to have a difficult time with the issue of "commitment" in a relationship. Since my husband and I have a happy forty-six-year marriage under our belt, they seem to consider us experts. It always irritates me when people tell us how "lucky" we are. Neither my husband nor myself consider our marriage a by-product of "luck." We have been "blessed" because GOD put us together. "Hard work" is how we feel we have stayed together all these years; but more importantly, it is how we have been happy also. We try (not always perfectly) to be aware of each other's needs and to remember that the little notes, unexpected flowers, and – most of all – kindness are just as important now as when we first married.

True love is given unconditionally and without a great many selfish expectations. Expectations seem to dwindle the longer people are together. Unconditional love has no expectations. Love does not keep score but keeps on being available and dependable – no matter what circumstances occur.

Real love gives its best and asks nothing in return. However, when someone is given unconditional love, the recipient can hardly refrain from receiving a warm feeling that eventually will make him want to respond in kind.

Love implies total commitment flowing to and from the parties involved. This commitment is present in the good times and the bad times, and mutual encouragement is mandatory. Only as we focus on the wonderful qualities that first attracted us to someone instead of looking for the bad are we able to see that person through "the eyes of love."

MY RICH

You ask me what love is, and I smile a quaint smile.
I'll tell you about my love if you have awhile.

The man that GOD gave me is so special, you see.
He's a prince among men and the whole world to me.

He's short and he's pudgy – with faults like us all;
But to his family and me, he's at least ten feet tall.

He is loving and tender; he is giving and sharing.
We're always aware of his constant caring.

He works very hard, but he seldom complains.
He never mentions his aches and his pains.

No matter how bad the situation may be,
He holds his head high and promises me:

"Tomorrow's a new day; and if you just trust,
Everything will be fine. We'll make it or bust."

My "Rock of Gibraltar," this special man,
Can make me believe by taking my hand

And saying he needs me – no matter what bumps
My life runs across and I'm down in the dumps.

Some call him a fool because he's a soft touch,
But this is one reason I love him so much.

His children respect him; he's always their friend.
On his love and his help, they can always depend.

He has a kind word for each one he might meet –
From dear friends to strangers he sees on the street.

He is a Christian; it shows in his living.
His sweet, loving spirit is constantly giving.

If I had the chance, there's no way I would switch
Because to me the word "LOVE" is the man I call "Rich."

THE MEADOW

*O*ne day as I was talking with a group of ladies, we got into a conversation about "the GOD of our understanding." We talked about our individual concepts of GOD as we pictured HIM.

When I was younger, my concept of GOD was very ambiguous. Although I was always told in church that "GOD IS LOVE," I also got the impression that HE was so large and busy with really important problems that the little things in my life were ridiculous and unimportant to HIM.

I felt HE did keep a halfhearted eye on me so that if I did something wrong HE could punish me. Unless my back was totally against the wall, I felt God was like a fire extinguisher case that said, "Break glass in case of emergency."

Fortunately, after I was grown (physically and chronologically), someone explained GOD'S true nature to me. He explained that MY GOD could be with me all the time. He told me He was loving and caring and interested in everything about me. He asked me to write a "job description" for the kind of GOD I would be comfortable with, and that is what I could have. I did that; and now – rather than being a punishing and stern parent, HE is a kind, loving FATHER who accepts me right where I am and loves me too much to let me stay there. HE is now a loving friend that I am comfortable sharing everything with. We talk off and on all day long.

One of the ladies in the group – with a great deal of spirituality – painted a word picture of her concept of GOD in her life, and it was beautiful. As I kept remembering this picture over and over, GOD led me to put it in the following poem form. Thanks, Andy, I love you!

THE MEADOW

I dreamed I was a little child
In a meadow green and grand.
I stood in great amazement,
For God held my tiny hand.

I did not know which way to run.
Each direction seemed so sweet;
But everywhere I tried to run,
Resistance I would meet.

I was in such a hurry
To get on with life and play;
But it seemed no matter how I tugged,
GOD would not let me stray.

He knew all the danger
That lurked along each path,
So HE stood firm and waited
'Til I vented all my wrath.

Finally in frustration,
I sat down to rest.
Then GOD began to move along
In the way HE knew was best.

I often lose direction.
GOD seems to move so slow;
But when I wait and let HIM lead,
I end up where I should go.

MY 'PEE POE'

*M*y father-in-law was a wonderful Christian man. He was always helpful and full of fun. "Pee Poe," as our older son nicknamed him, was eighty-six years young when GOD called him home. Chronologically, he was an old man; but he had a childlike spirit that made him a real joy to be around. Everyone who knew him loved him. He was a real southern gentleman.

He loved his children, grandchildren, and great-grandchildren and talked and laughed at and about their antics all the time. The only time I ever saw him really angry – even though he tried not to let it show – was when his long row of tomatoes he planted every year was at the stage when they were large but still green. We were all inside the house, and my younger son and his friend from next door – both around five or six years old – decided to use his tomatoes for a pretend battle they were having. When we went outside, only the new little tomatoes were left. They were hidden down low, but the almost ripe ones were totally unusable. When he saw it, he just turned and went back in the house. I am sure he was praying for the patience not to throttle them.

When he was diagnosed with colon cancer, we were all devastated. He lived for two years after his first surgery, but mostly his condition was going downhill. He was a fighter and loved life and managed to hang on longer than anyone expected. At the time of his death, he was only a shell of the body we had known; but he kept the same loving spirit that was his trademark.

I read the following poem as part of his eulogy. When I was asked how I could read it at the funeral, I explained that I felt this was the last thing I could do for him. This poem is dedicated to "Pee Poe" whom we all loved so dearly.

MY 'PEE POE'

I was eighteen years old when I met this man –
With the eyes so loving and kind.
I knew from his warm hug and welcome to me
That he'd be a great friend of mine.

He had no hair on that beautiful head,
But a smile on his face you'd expect –
With that famous cigar stuck in his mouth
And his clothing choice a little "suspect"!

His hands were so big and calloused and strong
Because hard work is what he knew best,
But he used them for GOD and all those he loved
When they were put to the test.

His laugh – so infectious – would make you believe
His life has been one long "ball."
Only those closest know the troubles he's known;
He has stood strong where others might fall.

His precious grandchildren were always his joy.
Their antics never seemed to get old.
He and the "Redhead" relived each detail
As with laughter the tales were retold.

Each Sunday we knew where "Pee Poe" would be.
His faith never waned or got cold.
He trusted his GOD and practiced his faith.
To let JESUS shine was his goal.

When his children had problems, we'd count on his prayers,
Asking GOD'S blessings on us.
His greatest concern was our spiritual lives,
Hoping in GOD we would trust.

As the years sped along, our relationship grew
Into something so very much more.
Like my own dad, he became an example of Christ
That I'd learned to love and adore.

When he was sick and feeling so bad,
I prayed it would help him to know
How he touched our lives in his own gentle way
And how much we all loved him so.

Whatever may happen in days lying ahead,
There is a promise that we all may share –
That "Pee Poe" who loved us and prayed for our souls
Will be waiting with open arms there.

THE CIRCLE

J am constantly amazed by the way GOD uses different events in our lives – some of them good and some of them seemingly so bad – to work HIS MAGNIFICENT PLAN in our lives. Each of us is comprised of the same inexpensive chemical elements, the same bones, the same organs, etc.; yet we are as individual as snowflakes.

Have you ever noticed when you are having an especially bad day that there always seems someone is put in your path who is having a good day? They encourage you and lift your spirits. This is no coincidence; it is all part of GOD'S plan.

HE puts us on earth to serve and encourage each other, to help those around us who are struggling, and to learn to accept help when we need it. This is how we grow. This ebb and flow of human frailty and strength is one of life's greatest blessings.

THE CIRCLE

Did you ever help a person
When they were really down –
Never even dreaming
That things might turn around?

You gave your love so freely
'Cause you had so much to share.
They were weak, and you felt strong;
So you showered them with care.

Then one dark day, you felt so low –
Life seemed too much to bear;
And the person who had once been weak
Was strong, and he was there.

In a flash, the roles reversed;
The teacher was the child.
He dried my tears, gave me a hug,
And helped my heart to smile.

In HIS WISDOM, our GOD knew –
If He would make us wise –
We'd have to have some dark days
To knock us down to size.

So if you are feeling strong today,
Then share it with a friend
'Cause tomorrow maybe he'll be strong
To help you once again.

AUNT WINNIE'S APRON

*M*y mother had two sisters. To say they were all different would be a gross understatement. Sometimes it seemed impossible to believe they were from the same planet – much less the same family. They were all wonderful people, and I loved each one of them very much. They were all unique and special in their own way.

Mother was outspoken but not as fiery as my Aunt Glennis. Needless to say, I doubt either of them would have made the diplomatic service. My mother wore her feelings on her sleeve. She could dish it out, but she could not take it very well.

My Aunt Glennis could go ballistic and tell you exactly how she felt about you without mincing any words at all. Ten minutes later, she was over it and sweet as could be. She never could understand why anyone was upset with her. She was one of the most generous people I have ever known. When she died, people came in droves to the funeral. They told us story after story about how she had helped each of them on various occasions. The numbers of floral arrangements were unbelievable.

Then there was my Aunt Winnie. She was ten years older than my mom and thirteen years older than Glennis. Because of the age difference, she seemed more like my grandmother than my aunt. She was sweet and soft-spoken and never had a bad word to say about anyone. For instance, I remember when Elvis Presley first appeared on "The Ed Sullivan Show"; and the whole world was "all shook up" about his gyrations and pelvic movements. Aunt Winnie said rather adamantly – for her, "He seems like a nice, sweet boy to me."

She had to be a saint to put up with all the antics from all us kids. There was a factory in town that made sandals with wooden soles, and each summer we all got a new pair. We would run through the house and up and down the uncarpeted stairs without even a reprimand. We adored Aunt Winnie; and when my children came along, they felt the same way.

I recall one time when were at her house and my son wanted a piece of cake. I said, "You have to go ask Aunt Winnie first." Looking back over his shoulder (he was about five), he said, "You be cutting it, while I go ask her." They got her number very quickly.

If she was at home, she was wearing an apron. If she dressed up to go somewhere to visit, she always had an apron with her; so she could help the hostess in the kitchen. It was such a family joke about that apron that her daughter lovingly put a clean, crisp apron in her casket.

Aunt Winnie was a special person and very, very loved. Heaven is a better place because she's there.

AUNT WINNIE'S APRON

From the moment she opened the door,
You saw love shining out from her face.
She was always happy to see you;
You were "home" when you entered this place.

Her hair was rolled up on top of her head;
Her housedress was cheery and bright;
But the thing you were sure you would see
Was an apron – usually flowered and white.

She always had something good to say
About everyone that she could.
If somebody else said something unkind,
She'd find something that she thought was good.

She petted us when we were sick;
Her sweet, loving touch was so real.
Better than medicine we might take,
We felt her tender touch could heal.

Wearing fine clothes for the holidays,
In someone's kitchen she also would wear

That clean, fresh apron that she would bring.
She took one everywhere.

When dressed for heaven and her reward,
She looked so beautiful and so neat;
But nestled in her casket
Was an apron in her hand so sweet.

Even though in heaven
She will be an honored guest;
She would not be happy
Without this last request:

"I have been YOUR servant, LORD,
On earth for many years.
I've had lots of happiness,
And I've shed many tears.

"But if YOU ever need help, LORD,
How quickly I will stand.
I'll be ready for YOUR SERVICE
With my apron in my hand."

SPIRIT OF CHRISTMAS PAST

*C*hristmas has always been a very special time for me. A large family always surrounded me, and we thoroughly enjoyed these times together.

When I was very young, I can remember that we all gathered at my aunt's home on Christmas Eve. There might be twenty or twenty-five of us who spent the night. My younger brother and I would be put to bed early in a bedroom upstairs that just happened to be right over the kitchen. I still recall the muffled chatter and the wonderful smells that wafted from the kitchen. We tried to stay awake to wait for Santa; but of course, we always fell asleep.

The excitement and anticipation of Christmas morning were almost too much for us to bear, but somehow we survived. We woke everyone at the crack of dawn to see what wonderful treasures Santa had left.

As we grew older and the families grew, Christmas traditions changed; but the love and the spirit and the people didn't, and it was still wonderful. The combination of the fantastic food and mostly the fellowship with loved ones made it the same – even though it was different.

Many of the people I remember from back then have died and gone on to their rewards. Just because things change, it does not cancel a particularly happy memory.

It reminds me that life is "change," and we must accept whatever that change brings because as we all learn: "Life goes on!" So many precious children have been added to our family. The joy they bring helps to fill the void of the loved ones we have lost.

Thank You, FATHER, that I have so many happy memories of family and holidays. It is hard not to be a little sad because of deaths and other changes, etc.; but happy memories are not limited to one particular time or place. We can make new ones every day. One of my college English professors gave us a quote I have never forgotten because it is so true: "GOD gives us memories, so we may have ROSES in December." I have been allowed so many ROSES in my life, and I am so thankful that each one is a wonderful memory stored in my heart.

SPIRIT OF CHRISTMAS PAST

"Home for the holidays" – what a beautiful sound!
A place where real joy and love still bound.

My memory takes me to days long ago;
I recall all the faces of those I love so.

It seems that their spirits still are so near –
Especially at home with the holidays here.

'Ole Sam, our dog, greets each one at the door;
He likes to share in the fun that's in store.

There's a tree that my dad took the kids out to get.
It's touching the ceiling; Ma's having a fit.

The smells from the kitchen are fragrant rare;
The aunts and the cousins are all gathered there.

My dear sweet aunt's apron is starched fresh and clean;
On her dress, plain or fancy, that apron is seen.

My cousin and I are cutting fruit in a bowl;
We'd laugh and keep cutting all it would hold.

One of my cousins was out delivering toys,
Helping poor folks and their girls and boys.

One of my cousins brought gifts for the tree.
"Hope the cooks all remember – NO ONIONS for me!"

I can see all the kids in their new cowboy suits,
Stomping around in their big cowboy boots.

My brother and his wife gave us a call
To say, "Merry Christmas" and send love to all.

My son got a fire truck with ladders and bells.
He's driving us crazy, but he thinks it is swell.

My husband has his coffee and is reading a book –
Either reading or eating anytime that we look.

Some cousins come late; they arrive in a flurry of:
"We can open the presents! Come on, ya'll. Let's hurry!"

My younger cousins were happy, of course;
I think they had gotten some things for their horse.

An uncle stacks gifts, unopened, no joy,
Until he gets to mine – he knows it's a toy!

My brother carved turkey – always ably assisted;
The urge for a sample was never resisted.

When we finally sat down, I can hear Daddy say,
"DEAR LORD, bless each family represented today!"

One aunt always fussed as she unzipped her dress:
"I just want one bite," but she'd finish the rest.

When dinner was finished, you'd hear her voice ring:
"Gather around the piano. We've carols to sing."

One cousin just rocked; he loved to rock so.
My uncle wore his hat; he was ready to go!

Ma's dishes were washed; there were presents to pack,
Knowing this special day would never be back.

But we have to be happy with our hearts full of joy
Because one of my cousins has a sweet baby boy.

And in not very long, his memories will be
Our present good times. LIFE GOES ON, DON'T YOU SEE?

MY SISTER LEAH

*W*hen I was growing up, I did not have a blood sister. However, I had a first cousin, Leah, who always has been more of a sister to me than a real sister ever could.

Like me, Leah had only brothers. Because we were the only two girls in the family, we "bonded" before I was even aware of what that meant.

She is a few years older than I am, but she always looked much younger. My children were always quick to point this out – especially after my hair turned white. They repeatedly commented there must be something wrong with the records about our ages. Children are "painfully honest," but I finally decided how to make them understand why she still looks so young. I said, "The reason she looks so much better and younger than I do is simple. SHE NEVER HAD CHILDREN!" This response shut them up at least temporarily.

Leah always has been a big part of my life. We have enjoyed many happy times and suffered through many sad times together. Because of this special relationship, these times were either twice as happy or half as sad due to the fact we had each other. Often we had to cling very closely. I was in the room with her mother, my Aunt Winnie, when she died; and as fate would have it, she was with my mother, her Aunt Jewell, when her time came to go.

My cousin has never let me down; and when I make a gratitude list, she is always very near the top. I know if I am sick, worried about my children, or just need a compassionate shoulder on which to cry, she is always there. I depend on her prayers because she most likely has a "HOT LINE" to OUR HEAVENLY FATHER.

This poem is my feeble attempt to let her know how much she is loved. I want her to know how much she has always and will always mean to me. It seems she has ESP and knows exactly when to call. Thank you for being my guardian angel. I love you, Sis.

MY SISTER LEAH

GOD gave me two brothers,
But He knew I needed more;
So He gave me a "substitute,"
A cousin I adore.

She's a little older,
But her looks would never show it.
She's beautiful – both in and out;
Her thoughtful actions show it.

Our families were so intertwined
We children never knew
We had several parents
And brothers by the slew.

We were together for the happy times;
We clung closely through the sad.
The love we shared helped every time
Through the good times and the bad.

She is always there to listen
When I need a loving ear.
When I have problems or I'm sick,
Her help and prayers are near.

When I count my blessings
And start to write my list,
One of the things right at the top
Is a "thank you" for "My Sis."

BRUISED EGO

*I*t was once such a chore for me to pray. I always had a burning desire to pray for the correct things for everyone I loved. Because of this difficulty, I was asleep, frustrated, or totally exhausted before my prayers were finished.

I had the mistaken idea that GOD was some sort of ethereal "short-order cook," patiently waiting for me to give HIM my order for the day. I'm still embarrassed when I realize how arrogant I must have been.

Prayer finally became such an odious and time-consuming task that I just quit praying – always with the idea of doing it later. I felt very guilty about it but not enough to attempt it again.

One Sunday at church, I heard the minister read the verse in the Bible that says we do not have to know for what to pray. It was such a relief to realize my prayer should be only that GOD'S WILL be done in my life as well as in the lives of all the others I included in my prayer time. Now I simply pray for GOD to give us what we need, and HE DOES!

Because of the freedom I found in this kind of praying, I now talk with GOD all through the day. I thank HIM for my many blessings and ask HIM to give me the courage to do HIS WILL as HE reveals it to me.

As with any relationship, it becomes more intimate and natural by investing my time and attention to learning more about HIM. Much to my chagrin, I have noticed things work out much better for everyone when I get out of the way and let GOD DO HIS WORK. At the expense of my ego, my prayer life – as well as all other areas of my life – become amazingly simple when I remember GOD IS IN CHARGE!

BRUISED EGO

Isn't It funny, isn't it strange
That GOD in HIS WISDOM could plan and arrange
The stars in the heavens, the tides of the sea;
Yet I'd feel HE needs someone finite as me

To help order the universe and help ease the strife –
Even though I can't handle mistakes in my life!
I feel I must hold every soul in my care
Without even a thought if HE wants me there.

If Joe is having a problem or Mary's not good,
I feel I'm not doing all that I should.
I put myself down, thinking something is wrong
If "Life's Choir" is not singing in tune to my song.

After awhile, there's a kick in my rear;
And I hear a heavenly voice in my ear:
"Calm down, My child. Stop spinning your wheels.
I'm quite sufficient to handle these deals.

"Just let it go, and in no time you'll see
Things are not such a mess if you give them to ME!
Why can't you remember before you're torn apart
That MY HELP'S always there right from the start?

"At the risk of bruising that EGO of yours,
My WISDOM is timeless and always endures.
Without your help – though it drives you to tears,
I've been running this world for quite a few years!"

LIFE'S CYCLE

I am certain there are those who would not agree with me; but other than my "SALVATION," I feel GOD'S greatest gifts to me are my children. We receive these children as a potter would receive a lump of clay. With GOD'S help, we are given the awesome task of molding them into loving, productive, and responsible members of society.

They do not come with an instruction manual. Most of us are ill prepared to begin to know how to tackle this monumental responsibility.

Much of the time parenting is tiring and thankless. We never know for sure if we are doing it well.

Young parents have asked me on several occasions how to rear a child. My answer has been: "Children are like little images of ourselves. They give back what they have been given. If they are shown love and respect, then that is what they give back. Unfortunately, if they are given verbal abuse and told they will not amount to anything, that is what they will give back. Most children's self-esteem is formed by the time they are out on their own. Sometimes with proper counseling, it can be overcome; but the tapes of their childhood play and replay constantly. Good tapes can lead to a successful life; while bad tapes can rob them of the potential they have, and they always seem to fail."

Other than that, the only advice I would give is to PRAY a lot. We try to do our best, and we have to leave the results to GOD.

Just when we are most confused and wonder how we have done at parenting, GOD gives us a gift that lets us know that – even with all of our mistakes – our child has grown into the kind, loving, self-respecting person we prayed he would become. This poem is about one such moment. I love you Dave!

LIFE'S CYCLE

Today my son and I walked in the woods
On some land he was thinking of buying.
The day was beautiful, the weather just right;
But the long walk was grueling and trying.

As I walked behind him, I fought to keep up
To prove I'm still one of the "guys";
But he wasn't fooled; he knew I was tired.
He was kind, but it showed in his eyes.

My mind wandered back to when he was a child,
And we tromped through the woods as today.
The scene I remember – quite different from this –
I recall as only child's play.

If I saw briars then, I cleared the path;
So he wouldn't be scratched or scarred.
Today his large foot pushed briars away,
So his mom's hands wouldn't be marred!

Oft in past walks, I had slowed my pace;
So his short, little legs could go slow.
Today it was he saying, "Mom, let's rest!"
He said HE was tired, but I know

He was saving my face as he took my hand
To help through rough spots in the way.
He said, "Just take your time. You're doing fine" –
My words on that long-ago day.

He took the time to point out little things –
Turtle shells and wild muscadines.
He showed me a spider spinning his web
And tracks where deer left their signs.

He told me to "Listen"; and dumbly I said,
"My darling, I don't hear a thing."
"Close your eyes, Mom, and listen again.
You'll hear crickets and birds as they sing!"

The present returns; and that dear, little boy
Is again a sweet, loving man,
Thanking GOD I've been blessed with children so fine –
My pride almost too much to stand.

My body is scratched and bruised and sore,
But my joy takes away all the pain
As I marvel again how GOD'S CYCLE goes on
And makes this old world almost sane.

So if you try your best when your children are young,
Your rewards will come back hundredfold
Because they become strong – yet gentle and kind –
And care about YOU when you're old!

HEALING THE CHILD

*T*here has been great controversy in the last several years about the "inner child" and whether it really exists. Some people spend long periods of time – as well as a great deal of money – with therapists, trying to sort out the effects of things that happened to them in childhood as a catalyst for their adult behavior. Therapists have long been going back to one's childhood to provide a reason for either positive or negative behavior that is displayed long after their childhood years.

Personally, although I feel we need to explore our childhood and make as much peace with it as possible, I also feel that sometimes people use their childhood as a "catch-all" to blame for childish or negative approaches to events in their lives. It has been a real struggle for me to try to learn to differentiate between when my behavior is "childish," which is manifested in selfish, uncaring, and petulant ways, or when I am being "childlike" with the faith, fearlessness, and trust that accompanies it.

Many times – after much soul searching, I am developing an awareness of which mode I am in at any given time. Physically and intellectually, I am a grown woman; while emotionally I sometimes slip into the wrong mode. I find I am always miserable until I grow up and face issues as an adult – even when the realities I must face are not pleasant.

In my experience, I have found that as I grow spiritually, God heals the hurt of my "childish" personality and integrates it into the "childlike" adult He wants us to be. Only God can bring about this integration and let the two coexist peacefully.

HEALING THE CHILD

There's a little girl I know
Who lives inside of me.
I'm trapped between this little girl
And the woman I should be.

Because of many unfair things,
This child could never grow;
So she just hid out deep inside,
So perhaps no one would know.

This child has always felt so small,
Unloved, and unprotected.
When she got hurt, she'd take control
In a way adults rejected.

The little things so cute at two –
When her tantrums she would wage –
Were at my age so out of place
They filled everyone with rage.

The more they turned away from her
This woman – still a child,
The more she tried to get her way
With acts and thoughts quite wild.

Neither liked the way they were –
Trapped in this dual role,
Caught in this constant struggle
Of who'd be in control.

This woman loved this little girl.
She'd felt her hurt, you know.
"She's MY CHILD. I'll care for her.
Let go so you can growl"

I mourn this child who lived in me –
Though most faults on her I blame;

But she's been there so many years
I can't help but feel her pain.

I pray that God will give me strength
To leave this child behind.
It will be hard, and she'll come back
To haunt from time to time,

To try to gain re-entrance
And beg I let her in.
Only God can help me
Know she is not my friend.

Grown woman that God makes me –
He will help me shut the door.
"Go away please, little girl.
You don't live here anymore!"

Please help me know the difference
As we are torn apart –
When I am being childish
Or just feeling "young at heart"!

Help me have a childlike faith
In YOU because YOU'RE strong,
Yet take away the childish "self"
That always guides me wrong.

I want to keep the childlike "awe"
That only YOU can give.
I want to have YOU hold my hand
Each day that I may live.

So take the frightened child inside
And teach her not to lie.
Then I can't use her anymore;
And I can say, "Goodbye!"

MY LITTLE GIRL

*U*ntil my daughter was born, there had not been a girl born in the Poe family in thirty years. I wanted a little girl very badly, but I was afraid to even hope that it might really happen.

I already had a little boy, and he was wonderful; so I had resigned myself to the fact that the child I was carrying would be son number two. I was so convinced that I already had picked out the name "Danny" to go with "David," my number-one son.

I always have had very open and satisfying relationships with my boys, and we got along really well; but Tam was a different story. No one had bothered to tell me there is an unwritten law that declares as girls reach adolescence they become natural enemies of their mothers. They feel duty bound to disagree about everything their moms say, do, or suggest. If a mom says it is "white," the daughter automatically takes the position that it is "black".

Tam spent her teenage years in her room with the door locked, so she could have her privacy as she talked on the phone for hours. She came out for meals, school, and dates; but otherwise, we didn't see much of her.

Only after she was married and had a daughter of her own did she begin to realize I was not as old fashioned as she had thought. Tam and I are great friends now, sharing a mutual love and respect. Every year I send her the same Mother's Day card. It has a frazzled, young mother looking at her daughter's messy room as her daughter hangs on the phone. The message inside simply says, "Now you know!"

I am very proud of the mom she is now and the way she has always been. She is always there for me, and I consider her one of God's sweetest gifts. I love you very much TAM!!

MY LITTLE GIRL

"Boys run in my family,"
My husband told me.
"You won't have a girl.
Just you wait and see!"

I had a fine son whom I loved very much
And was really a "boy" to the bone;
But still I longed for a doll to dress—
A sweet, little girl of my own.

When delivery came, I was truly shocked,
The feeling was really uncanny.
I had my darling, cuddly girl
Not the boy already named "Danny."

She stole my heart from the moment of birth
'Cause she was so precious and small.
I was NUMBER TWO in my husband's heart now,
But that made no difference at all.

She was "Daddy's Princess" who made him feel
That he was the king of the world;
But though we had differences – as is often the case,
Deep down she was her "Mama's Girl!!"

Her teenage years were spent in her room;
She was usually glued to her phone.
She had lots of friends; but strangely enough,
She preferred to spend much time alone.

When she got married, I know for a fact
She was the world's most beautiful bride.
As she came down the aisle on her father's arm,
My tears were mixed with my pride.

The years brought her troubles – some of them rough;
But these times brought us closer, you know.
We cried together and clung very close;
Trouble made our relationship grow.

Now she has a daughter, the joy of her life.
She now understands and can see
How I must have felt when she came along
'Cause now she's NUMBER TWO and I'm THREE.

MY PRAYER

*G*od uses poetry to speak to me. Through this poetry, if God inspires it, I become willing to offer my "free will" back to God; so HE can call the shots. In doing His will, we can – if we are willing to go through the pain necessary to grow – be happy, joyous, and free in our life. Each day I pray only for the knowledge of God's will for me and the COURAGE to carry it out just for that day because that day is all I have.

I have heard it said, "Yesterday is a canceled check; tomorrow is a promissory note; and today is the only cash we ever have." Whenever I let go and ask for God's guidance, it always comes in God's time – not mine; but it always comes!!

MY PRAYER

My heart is breaking, LORD;
I'm shaking with fright.
Not much in my life
Seems to be going right!

God, I need the peace
That comes only from YOU;
But there are so many things
I'm not willing to do.

My brain keeps on churning;
I project my worse fears
'Til finally I give way
And break down in tears.

Over and over,
I've been told what to do.
I must give up my struggle,
Turn it over to YOU!

Please, Lord, take my will
That's so prideful and bold.
Change it and use it
For some heavenly goal.

Let these troubles I'm having
Work for my good
To accomplish the purpose
Only YOU know they should.

Like a loved child that's punished,
Please help me to see
Painful growth makes me stronger
And means YOU love me!

God, help me to find that quiet middle ground
Where peace and serenity flow.
Alter my will, and use it for you;
So my life Your glory will show.

The beautiful glow that Your peace can bring
Can shine from the most homely face.
God, grant me Your peace and that heavenly glow
Only YOU in Your Wisdom can place.

Dear Lord, make me willing
In each part of my life to always let You have Your Way,
Asking only for strength and guidance from YOU
That I will require for today.

I THINK I'LL RUN AWAY

*M*y three-year-old son was angry with me. With his childish mentality, he had decided to run away – with absolutely no thought or preparation. When I saw the determined look in his eye, it made me sad to think many times this is the way I am perceived by GOD. My child's actions were not unlike my own when I want to be in control and I figuratively kick and scream and pitch a temper tantrum to try to get my own way.

Just as I was amused by the insanity of his attempt to run away, I was at the same time very sad that he was so unhappy. It was so obvious to me that my child's unhappiness was of his own making and that he had the power to turn the situation around anytime he chose. The same is true in my own case; suffering ceases at the moment I give up the struggle.

Our HEAVENLY FATHER does not enjoy seeing us in pain; and when we give up the fight, HE will gather us in HIS ARMS and give us HIS LOVE and HIS PEACE. I love you Russ; and I'm glad you didn't run away!

I THINK I'LL RUN AWAY

When my son was only three,
We had a great big row.
He hated me and was leaving home;
I could hardly wait to see just how.

He found a great, big moving box
The largest size they make.
Even through his tears and anger,
He knew he had lots of stuff to take.

He emptied all his chest of drawers,
Piled in all the toys that he could see.
He only left his toothbrush
'Cause he thought that might hurt me!

When the box was overflowing,
He still looked quite defiant,
Forgetting that to move that box
Would take the JOLLY 'OLE GREEN GIANT.

THE HEALING BED

He struggled, and he pushed and shoved
And screamed – he was so mad.
To see all this frustration
Made his "mama" very sad.

So I knelt down, gave him a hug,
And held him very tight.
At first, he fought to pull away
But soon gave up the fight.

I told him how much I loved him.
As I helped him put away
All of his possessions,
I said how glad I was he stayed.

I read him his favorite story
In my lap snug and secure
Just another childhood crisis
We both had to endure.

Late that night, I lay in bed,
Remembering our fray
And thought how very like my child
I acted every day.

I, too, am often tempted to try to run away
When I am acting childish and things don't go my way.
I moan and struggle, complain and cry;
Then I hear my FATHER say,

"Enough, My child, I love you so.
I cannot let you go.
The times you feel I do not care
My love for you will grow.

"So put away your childish toys
And rest upon My breast
Because whatever you must face,
MY LOVE will pass the test.

"Just trust in ME and you will find
You always will succeed.
You may not get each thing you WANT
But EVERYTHING YOU NEED!"

FREE CHOICE

*W*hen I am thinking rationally, I realize one of the most beautiful gifts GOD gives us is that of "CHOICE" or "FREE WILL." This wonderful power of choice is what separates us from the animals, gives us a soul, and makes us in GOD'S IMAGE.

Some days when I am struggling with the results of some bad choice or choices I have made, I question whether we wouldn't be better served to be like the animals that live by instinct. They just do what comes naturally to them without having to think about it or make a decision. However, when I settle down and regain my perspective, I know the quality of our lives and our very souls will live forever, depending on that marvelous gift of "CHOICE."

God does, however, give us instincts that make us realize we must seek a power higher than ourselves to have happy, useful, and productive lives. He also furnishes us with an intellect that recognizes the "GOD-SHAPED HOLE" in each of us can be filled only by HIS LOVE and SPIRIT! The following poem is about our power to choose.

FREE CHOICE

God, You are so loving,
So helpful, and so kind.
Why do I always struggle
And stagger like I'm blind?

Why don't You just shake me
And let me hear You say,
"All you need for happiness
Is to do things like I say!"

But I guess we'd never learn
If You took away our choice.

We'd just be like puppets,
And we'd have no real voice.

I guess all the wear and tear
Is the price that we must pay
To be fit to live in heaven
And be with YOU one day.

My life just gets so miserable
Cluttered up with fear again.
I need a good house cleaning.
Please take out all the sin.

All I can see are the bad things
As I struggle on my way.
I forget to pause and thank You
That my blessings far outweigh.

My life just gets so filthy
With self-pity and with pride.
Headstrong, I just plunge right in,
Forgetting You're my guide.

Away from the winds and the jagged rocks
That batter me and bruise,
I forget to ask for YOUR STRENGTH
That's there if I would choose.

Like the manna sent from heaven
That came each and every day,
Likewise we must seek YOUR WILL
Exactly the same way.

Please, Father, take my pride;
Get me out of YOUR WAY.
Help me know what I should do
Today and every day.

FREE AT LAST

*I*t is hard for me to really remember the pain I suffered for so many years. As the pain of childbirth fades because of the joy it brings, so it is with spirituality. As I learn through daily practice how much easier our lives become and what freedom "letting go and letting GOD" brings, I tend to forget the struggle and daily warfare in which I was once engaged every single day of my life. When I speak with someone who is in the midst of the struggle, I am reminded of those desperate feelings of antagonism, unhappiness, fear, and self-loathing I suffered before I began to find the better way.

I was truly an EGOMANIAC with an INFERIORITY COMPLEX. I felt no one could handle things but me; yet in the deep recesses of my mind, where there was a glimmer of REALITY, I knew I could not handle things either. Constant struggle was the order of every day. One voice was shouting I was responsible; while another was shouting just as loudly how I was inferior and inept.

I spent exhausting hours trying to decide what everyone needed; so if I couldn't handle it, I could pray and tell GOD what to do. I became a gracious and resentful martyr who was in constant pain. Only resorting to my various addictions could numb that pain. I felt I must CARE for everyone, PLEASE everyone, and TURN all my resentments and anger inward.

In the Bible, we are told to "love thy neighbor as thyself." I slowly began to realize if I was as harsh and critical to my neighbor as I was to myself – I would probably be in jail.

It was a real turning point in my life when I finally realized that GOD intended me to care for myself first. I deserve more than the crumbs left over after taking care of others. It was a complete turnaround for me. I had always been taught you should place everyone else first and if anything was left – you could have it. Slowly, I accepted the concept that only as I first care for myself can I truly be of use to GOD, my fellowman, or myself. As this concept – through practice – became more natural, the opposing voices in my head became one that agreed that taking care of myself is not selfish but GOD'S PLAN. Only by experiencing this truth for myself could I know the incredible sense of light-heartedness and freedom that is and always has been at my disposal.

FREE AT LAST

For years there was a battlefield
Locked up within my soul
Where struggle raged every day
As to what really was life's goal.

The face I showed the public
Was happy and inspiring.
Even those who knew me best
Felt I was worth admiring.

I anticipated needs I filled
Folks never knew they had.
I never thought about myself –
Except as worthless and so bad.

I felt I was a martyr –
Unselfish as could be,
Never realizing my motive
That now those folks "owe" me!

Part of me felt oh so smart;
No one could do so well.
Another part felt insecure,
So my heart stayed in its HELL!

My ego was so very large.
It pushed me on ahead;
While underneath I was afraid.
I wished that I were dead.

My theory was quite simple –
At least it seemed to me:
If I took care of everyone,
They should take care of me.

I was hurt so many times;
Those I'd helped did not come through.
I knew I could not help myself,
So what was I to do?

Then one day I finally stopped
And heard my FATHER'S VOICE.
This time I did not run away –
As in the past had been my choice.

"You are MY CHILD – with all your faults.
MY LOVE can make you free.
Don't put your faith in others.
What you need must come from ME!

"You don't have to have this battle
That keeps tearing you apart.
If you are only willing,
I'll put peace in your scarred heart."

HE has never let me down so far;
I know HE never will.
HE gave me a freedom
Each day on which to build.

I pray each day that those I meet
HIS LOVE in me will see;
But their happiness depends on GOD,
So I am free to just be me.

VULNERABLE? YOU BET!

*M*y son's first child, a daughter, was born at 9 p.m. by cesarean section. Since I am a Registered Nurse, he and I both were privileged to be present in the operating room during the procedure. My son was stationed behind the drape to give support to his wife; but being used to the operating arena and being filled with excitement, I was allowed to stand at the foot of the table. I was able to see my granddaughter immediately as she was born and let out her first yowl!

I had the distinct honor of being the first one in our family to hold this precious new life. The pediatrician wrapped her in a blanket after he pronounced her perfect; then gave her to me. I gave her to her mom and dad. It was a beautiful and spiritual event, and I will always be grateful I could participate.

My son was floating on a cloud. Occasionally, he would make an obligatory visit to his wife; but he spent the rest of the night at the nursery window – in awe of the new, little miracle.

He is still in awe of his little girl and her younger brother who is two and a half years her junior. I remember vividly the first time she became ill. He experienced that fear only the parent of a sick child can feel. As we talked, I realized he had joined the ranks of a club peculiar to parents. I knew he would be a member until the day he died. Trials and joys accompany membership, but it is worth the trials to get the joys.

VULNERABLE? YOU BET!

I tried to tell you, my precious child,
How vulnerable you would be –
From the moment they're born 'til the day you die
And they lay you beneath some oak tree.

The first time you see them, your heart starts to swell
In a place where rare love exists.
Things are never the same; they never can be.
You know with that very first kiss.

This miraculous gift – so helpless and warm –
Has made you her servant for life.
You're in this together – through thick and through thin,
The good times, the heartaches, the strife.

Each time they are sick, you stiffen with fear.
You imagine the worst that could be.
You pray and you fret and wish ten thousand times:
"Oh, LORD, WHY CAN'T IT BE ME?"

You think when they're little it will be better soon
When childhood frustrations are o'er;
But your real trouble starts when they start to grow
And they go alone out the door.

You are so helpless; you have no control;
You wish they were little again.
This is the way GOD teaches us FAITH.
You must give them to HIM, my dear friend.

Your hair starts turning gray; they do things you don't like.
They have faults oh so hard to forget;
And just when you think all your work is for naught,
They say, "Gee! You're the best daddy yet!"

So remember the journey – so hard and so long –
Has many surprising rewards.
They aren't usually riches, silver or gold,
But the character you've been working toward.

You get what you give, remember, my child.
Faith, love, and respect are your prizes.
Do whatever it takes and make them believe
They cannot fail in your eyes.

So say lots of prayers, and give them your love.
Somehow it will bring you both through.
One thing keeps you sane when you're so afraid:
"GOD loves them a lot more than you!"

JOURNEY IN FAITH

O ccasionally, I feel I need to retrace some of my steps on my "JOURNEY IN FAITH" with my HEAVENLY FATHER. I suppose I would not be human if once in a while I did not slip back into the FEAR of economic insecurity. On such days, I just close my eyes and recall all the promises GOD gave us. He said, "I know what you need, and I will provide it on MY TIMETABLE in the way I think best."

When the way is smooth and everything in our life is mostly sunshine and flowers, it is easy to believe. It is in the darkness of night and trouble that I have twinges of apprehension. During these times of fear, the DEVIL is doing his dead-level best to take away my serenity. It is my choice whether I let him succeed or fail.

The Bible tells us: "In whatsoever state we find ourselves, we should be content." GOD absolutely insists HIS CHILDREN be HAPPY, JOYOUS, and FREE – no matter what is happening in the world around them.

I can remember many occasions when I had a lapse of faith, and it makes me stronger to recall the final outcomes of such lapses. Perhaps you might enjoy being ushered into the inner sanctum of my heart as I remember a few of these times.

*　　*　　*　　*　　*

As far back as I can remember, I suppose I was exposed to money issues. My mom and dad had a hard time making ends meet, and I would hear them discussing how they might handle these financial problems. Because my parents lived through the Great Depression, they were especially fearful about finances.

I can remember any talk about money was interpreted by me as "impending doom." I was so afraid that I never asked for anything because in my "magic magnifying mind," I felt it would be a hardship on my parents. I can remember my mom saying, "You never want anything!" If we went in a shop, she would want me to try on a dress and I would refuse.

Even at that tender age, I recognize I had the mind of an addict and I saw every situation out of proportion. I either saw it much better or much worse than those around me. Reality was never one of my choices.

*   *   *   *   *

When my husband and I got married, we had debts that completely devoured our combined incomes. He was twenty-one and had a salary of $250 a month. I was nineteen and had a salary of $175 a month.

We had been married for only a few months when I became pregnant with our first son. Shortly thereafter, I began to have health problems that made it necessary for me to stop working. It was a scary time.

My husband was going to college at night to get a second degree. He was attending school on the GI bill, but his checks had not begun to arrive.

It was his birthday, and I was accustomed to my family making a big fuss over birthdays; but we were 250 miles from my family, and his folks had forgotten and did not invite us to dinner. We had one can of English peas in the house, and I was very depressed. We were definitely not in a festive mood. However, when we arrived home that evening, his first GI check was waiting for us. We went to my husband's cousin's store and cashed the check. Then we bought fifty dollars worth of groceries (unheard of in 1954), and we went out to dinner.

GOD gave us what we needed! This was GOD'S LESSON in PATIENCE and how HIS TIMETABLE is often different from ours. Sometimes it seems SLOW, but it is never LATE!

*   *   *   *   *

One of my most memorable experiences in financial matters occurred while I was still working at the college and had first learned I was pregnant. One morning as my husband, who is a big-time coffee drinker, was in the shower, I checked his pockets and my purse and realized we had twenty-five cents between us. He already knew and had put it in my purse. Back then, I could get a bowl of soup and crackers for twenty-five cents in the college cafeteria. I knew he would not have coffee without the quarter, so I slipped it in his pants pocket. At noon (because I had no lunch money), I decided to take a walk. As I walked in front of the college, I looked up and there was my husband. He had made a twenty-mile round trip to bring me the quarter! He said, "You are eating for two, so go eat." Today I regret that I spent that quarter. As my marriage went on, I realized what a precious gesture that was!

I have a relative who GOD uses to bail me out from time to time by just dropping me a note with a check in it. The lesson GOD taught me in this situation was the beauty of LOVE and SACRIFICE.

*   *   *   *   *

I do not remember a time in my life when I felt I had money to waste, but some times have been more "flush" than others. When our youngest son was born, my husband was selling insurance on a strictly commission basis. We had a lousy medical insurance policy that paid seventy-five dollars (both doctor and hospital) in total. Since I required a C-section, they paid a whole $125. I was a Registered Nurse by then; but because of the pregnancy, I had not worked in several months and I could not go back to work for at least six weeks.

My husband came down with a severe case of the flu that required high-priced prescriptions, and our little savings were gone in a flash. He was unable – because of high fevers – to go back to work for nearly a month. I will never forget the day his commission check came in the mail; it was for two dollars. Talk about fear! There we were – two grownups, two young children, and a new baby.

My parents helped us survive. My mom and I would go to the grocery store, and she would get two shopping carts: one for them and one for us. I had no choice but to accept their help; and I remember her saying, "The way to pay me back is to do it for your children when they need it." We have since done that many times, and I realize now it was a pleasure for her to help us – just as it has been when we could help ours. This was GOD'S lesson in HUMILITY.

* * * * *

Because of my disability when I was so young, I only get a small check from Social Security Disability. I have Medicare, and I am truly thankful for both; but with all of the insurance and drug bills – as well as various doctors, things get really tight on occasion. We have a catering business, and it seems it is always feast or famine.

I give a tithe to my church because that is what GOD has told me to do, and I believe HE blesses that. I have tested this theory when my faith was weak, and I have realized I always end up worse financially when I fail to tithe.

One time when I was really struggling with the devil about whether to pay my tithe or keep it for bills, I took the high road and I mailed my tithe. I was sick at the time, and I knew of no way I could pay a necessary doctor bill and a prescription. Even though I have seen GOD work HIS WONDERS many times, I guess I am still a little amazed. I wrote checks for these things, and the total was sixty-nine dollars. When I got home and looked in the mailbox, there was an insurance reimbursement check for some other prescriptions for sixty-nine dollars and thirty-one cents! This occasion taught me the lesson that GOD may not feel I need any extra, but my NEEDS are always met.

* * * * *

I can cite case after case of GOD taking care of me and giving me what I needed when I asked, but I will close with one story that is so special to me that I have to relate it. In 1972 when we moved to Marietta, Georgia and moved our church membership to Roswell Street Baptist Church, we became members in March or April and the youth high school choir was going to Israel with the pastor and a group of other adults. They were going to sing in Bethlehem on Christmas Eve night. Just to think about it made the hair on my neck stand on end. In addition to my older son and daughter, we had another teenager who stayed with us most of the time and I also very much wanted him to have this opportunity for this once-in-a-lifetime experience.

There was one little "catch." All the other kids, who had been in the choir a long time, had done all kinds of projects to pay their way. It would cost $600 each for the trip, and the deadline for payment was the next Sunday. My husband and I were brokenhearted because we wanted the kids to go so badly. We prayed and asked GOD if it was HIS WILL for them to go to please show us a way. We remembered the Bible said, "Faith without works is dead"; so we all set out to work at raising money.

I remember the man with whom I rode to and from work with every day told me I was "NUTS" because we would never raise that much money in less than a week. My reply was: "If GOD wants them to go, HE WILL make a way!"

We called relatives and friends. We asked our employers for donations, and they all were generous. On the Sunday morning when the money was to be turned in, we were still three hundred dollars short. We all had to admit that the trip was not in GOD'S PLAN.

As we sat in Sunday school, we were very downhearted. A couple in our class spoke up and said they had sold some property, and they would like to use their tithe from the sale to help our kids make this trip. You probably already have guessed that they sold the property for $3,000, and their $300 tithe made the trip a reality instead of a dream!

It was lonely without our older children that Christmas; but they showed scenes of Bethlehem on TV, and my husband and I were so happy to think our children were worshipping in the very spot where the manger had been. It always will be remembered as our miracle Christmas. What a lesson in FAITH we learned – that our finite minds can only see one or two ways something can happen; while GOD has thousands of ways to do anything HE thinks is good for us and what we need.

Sometimes I get my priorities mixed up, and I forget that being RICH and being WEALTHY are two entirely different things. Being rich comes from inside and makes us happy because we have been blessed with family and friends who love us – even when we are dead broke. To be rich is to know THINGS are just that, and they do not make one truly happy. Being rich is knowing what we do for GOD and our fellowman are the only things of lasting value.

Many wealthy people are miserable trying to protect their money, and wealth is all they know. They miss the important things. While many people with riches do not realize how blessed they are, many people with wealth do not realize how miserable they are and always will be – with only tangible things to make them happy.

I have friends who play the lottery several times a week, and some asked me if I ever play. I was quick to reply that sometimes I am tempted; but deep down I know GOD knows WHAT and HOW MUCH I need, and I do not feel I can insult Him by trying to force HIS HAND. I have been a caretaker all my life; and I know if I had an unlimited supply of funds at my disposal, I could be the WORLD'S WORST ENABLER.

The lessons I have learned when I had to let go and TOTALLY depend on GOD could never have been learned any other way, and I do not want to be the cause of others not learning the lessons HE wants them to learn. My most precious memories have been made during the worst financial times. My husband of forty-six years and I agree these times were when we became the closest and clung to each other the tightest. As the song says, "I don't know about tomorrow. I don't claim to understand; but I know WHO holds the future, and I know WHO holds my hand!" I am truly RICH – no matter what my financial situation!

WELCOME TO MY WORLD

*M*y friend introduced me to the circus after I was a grown woman with a husband and three children. We traveled to Birmingham, Alabama to see the "Red Unit" of the Ringling Brothers and Barnum and Bailey Circus.

I had had a fusion of my neck, and I was still fastened in a metal brace. Just before the lights came up, my friend unlocked the side of my brace; so I could look up enough to get the full effect of what was about to happen.

As the house lights came up, I immediately became a child again, looking at the sawdust, sparkles, beautiful costumes, animals, clowns, web girls, hawkers, etc. – with an awe that nearly took my breath away. This poem was a birthday present to my friend in an attempt to say "thanks" for this wonderful gift he had given me that day. Thanks P. T.!!!

WELCOME TO MY WORLD

He said, "I know a place, a whole different world,
Where there's joy from beginning to end.
It's my special world; I admit very few;
But I'll take you because you're my friend."

When we reached this place of canvas and poles,
There were pleasures that I'd never known.
He smiled with delight at the look on my face –
A child again – even though grown.

Bright-colored balloons floated about;
Hawkers were peddling their wares.
Children and grown-ups all seemed the same.
This magic place took all their cares.

Even the smells in this marvelous place
Were different from any I knew –
Hot dogs with onions; popcorn, of course;
Cotton candy; and the animals too.

The music began (a march I believe);
The beautiful show came to life.
When the band started playing, it seemed to be saying,
"Forget all your frustration and strife."

Beautiful ladies dressed in pink tights
Flirted with death on their swings;
While acrobats, jugglers, equestrians too
Frolicked below in the rings.

There were flyers and elephants, wirewalkers too,
And animal trainers renown;
But the thing that tugged on my heartstrings the most
Was the sad-looking, lonely, ole clown.

My heart skipped a beat; tears of joy filled my eyes;
And joy overtook my whole being.
I could hardly believe this magnificent sight
That my childlike eyes were now seeing.

The finale was done, and we left that place.
I felt it had all been a dream,
But GOD in His goodness had sprinkled my heart
With SAWDUST as part of His scheme.

I watched as the "Roustabouts" loaded the train
And knew as the old whistle blew
That along with my gladness would always be sadness
That I couldn't load and go too!

I knew in my heart this was only the start
Of a fever from which there's no cure;
So I hope every day that I'll hear someone say,
"The circus is coming for sure."

People may change, gifts fade away,
Happy times come to an end;
But no one can take what he gave to me
On that spring day because he's my friend.

Gay S. Poe "AKA Princess T."

BATTLE OF THE BULGE

I have had a weight problem all of my life. Sometimes I feel like I weighed in at 125 pounds when I was born, but my mother assures me that was not the case.

I was a chubby child; and I learned very early that excess food – and especially sugar – could numb any emotions with which I did not want to deal. Even the emotions most people enjoy – such as savoring compliments, looking good, being humorous, or anything positive – were emotions that produced great fear and trepidation in my mind. Was this crazy thinking and unreasonable behavior? You bet it was; but it was very real to me, and it was years before I realized it was a disease over which I had no control.

Every week I would decide on Monday I would go on a strict diet and miraculously I would be thin in a couple of weeks – even though it had taken years to put on the weight. I would start out each Monday with a firm resolve; but by Monday night, I was nervous, irritable, and ready to do battle with anyone who was unfortunate enough to cross my path.

Now that I have a little sanity, I realize if I had just eaten sensibly on a daily basis I would not have gained all the weight. Then these weekly exercises in futility would not have been necessary. I now know overeating is an addictive disease – much like alcohol and drug abuse; and only God can take away this compulsion. This poem is the story of my life before I was fortunate enough to receive this realization.

BATTLE OF THE BULGE

Do you fight the war that I constantly wage –
The war against fat? It fills me with rage!

I try to ignore it and pretend it's not there,
But my mirror reveals it – especially when bare!

There are subtle, little hints that signal this fight;
For example, the shower curtain starts to get tight.

I announce to the world my steadfast conviction
That on my eating I'll put a restriction.

My family all cringes and says, "Oh! Not again!"
But this time I'll show 'em – this time I'll win!

I stuff all weekend and say it's O.K.
'Cause on Monday morning – boy, that is the day!

Monday morn comes, and I wake full of fight
Because, after all, I ate half the night.

I just won't think about food I say to myself,
While I try to forget chocolate cake on the shelf.

My breakfast was skimpy; I had it at eight.
I started my chores to forget about weight.

I tried exercise, but that's not for me;
So I settled down to watch some T.V.

I'm a little bit hungry, but I'm doing fine
'Til the wall clock reminds me it's not even nine!

I've made it to lunch; I have such a strong will.
Boy, this is hard! Can't I just take a pill?

I've bitten my fingernails down to the quick
And had so much celery it's making me sick!

I soaked in the tub 'til I looked like a prune,
Waiting for dinner and praying it's soon.

A cup full of cottage cheese – that was the fare,
And I gulped it all down without even a chair!

I went to bed early; maybe that was the cure;
But by midnight I'd had all that one could endure.

Ever so quietly, I slithered from bed
Straight to the kitchen — FULL STEAM AHEAD!

After three candy bars and a sandwich or two,
I had a diet cola – the least I could do!

As I crept back to bed – feeling guilty but grand,
My husband just smiled. He's a wonderful man!

So I blew it again, but this is just ONE day.
I promise you this; I'll lick it next Monday.

L I F E   L E S S O N S   F R O M

THE TEXAS TERMINATOR

*J*n a twelve-step program, your sponsor is next in the chain of command after God – if you use them properly. Because of our screwed-up thinking, we must have someone we can trust to run things by. Usually, this person has been involved in the program long enough to remember the tricks and lies we come up with because he has used them himself.

Many people look at me and see a sweet, little "blue-haired lady"; and they try to be gentle and kind. God knew that was not the kind of sponsor I needed. I thought I had my routine perfected, but it didn't take me long to realize if I didn't want to know his opinion, I better not ask for it. My age and the color of my hair did not get any points with "The Texas Terminator."

My first sponsor took me bodily to my first meeting and didn't pull any punches when he talked with me. He died in 1988, and I was sure I would never find anyone else who would know how to sponsor me; but God always provides us what we need if we really seek Him.

We have always had a love-hate relationship. Everyone who knows us both can't imagine how we can work together because we fuss and argue constantly; but when we are in the sanctity of the sponsor/sponsoree relationship, we really click. I almost never like what he is says, that is, "a cat is a better mother than you are" when he is explaining that I don't have to pad all the corners for my children. He has learned much patience from our relationship, and I have learned to be more truthful – both to him and to myself. Learning to be truthful (I never knew I lied to myself) has been one of the greatest gifts I have received.

I have learned that God loves me unconditionally and so does Frank – only he is much more vocal. I think I scare him because I am one of the few who has learned that under his rough exterior is one of the kindest, most spiritual men I have ever met. I thank God often that he is in my life.

THE TEXAS TERMINATOR

I am known for my hard head;
It couldn't be much harder.
I'll try anything to get my way;
With God I'll even barter!

One day God said, "I'm sick of her.
She really is a nut.
She thinks she can outlast Me,
But in Texas there's this 'butt.'

"He's hard as nails, mean as a snake.
He doesn't give an inch.
I'll put him in charge and challenge him
'Cause she won't be a cinch!"

My "blue-haired", sweet ole lady bit
Had worked well in the past;
But with this hardened "Con Man,"
He caught on really fast.

I used my best excuses,
And they all sounded sane;
But he would pick them all apart.
One by one, my lies he'd drain.

My perfect words of wisdom
He cut right down to size.
To say, "Yeah, but YOU DON'T UNDERSTAND!"
Began to seem unwise.

When someone asked a question
And my motives were all wrong,
I'd dazzle them with footwork
And make my answers long.

But I really learned frustration
As his wisdom he would show:
"Poe, don't filibuster.
The answer's 'Yes' or 'No'!"

God said, "I love that white-haired witch,
But I'm not always there to rate her;
So I'll send her the best I've got –
'The Texas Terminator!!!'"

I love you Frank.

EXAMPLE

*L*ike most people, I abhor hypocrisy. This is probably because in it I see so many of my own character defects. I try to deny them even to myself.

I have never done well accepting the premise that is so prevalent which says, "DO WHAT I SAY, NOT WHAT I DO." It always meant much more to me when someone had the "intestinal fortitude" to back up his or her words with like actions.

Though no one is ever perfect, once in awhile, GOD puts someone in my path to demonstrate what that means. It is someone – although not perfect – who attempts day after day to "WALK THE WALK" and not just "TALK THE TALK." These role models show us by example. From them, we learn how to live more honestly with those around us – as well as ourselves.

I will always appreciate the unlikely person GOD sent to "spoon feed" me spirituality and force me to swallow – no matter how much I resisted. It is the greatest gift anyone has ever given me. As I look back from my present vantage point, I only can imagine the love and patience it required and that was so freely given. That person is still my "example." Thank You, GOD, again for my "TEXAS TERMINATOR."

EXAMPLE

It has always been so hard for me
To do the things I should.
I want to take the high road,
But it seemed I never could.

THE FATHER'S ROAD is simple;
HE tells me what to do –
Simple, yet so very hard,
With twists and turns all new.

GOD said, "I'll give you a person
To help you on your way –
Someone who's been where you must go,
And I'll tell him what to say."

He talks to me and points it out
When I am out of line.
He forcefully reminds me
Of my faults to which I'm blind.

He could talk forever
If in him I could not see
YOUR LOVE and someone practicing
The life I want for me.

I've seen him in some bad times
When guilt and anger seared.
I've also seen him many times
Let go of things he feared.

Thank You for real people
Who don't just TALK the TALK.
Thanks for their "example"
As we see them WALK the WALK!

Sometimes mere words might slip right by.
We forget them as they pass;
But when we see them live the words,
The message seems to last.

Following directions is hard for me
Say friends who really know me.
If you expect to get results,
Then don't just tell me – SHOW ME!

If you believe the words you say,
Then let your actions show it.
I can't mistake what I have seen,
So then I'll really know it.

RESENTMENT

*R*esentment is a feeling of being wronged and replaying the incident over and over in our minds. We seem to get a perverse enjoyment out of reliving the incident, the people involved, their dialogue and ours –sometimes as it actually was but more often as we perceived it or wished it had been.

I have met many people whom I have heard say, "I wish I could just think fast enough to say what I wish I had said." My problem is just the opposite. I think too quickly, and the sarcastic words those people wish they could think of are already out of my mouth. I used to think of this as a real gift, and I thoroughly enjoyed bettering my peers with cutting sarcasm. As I mature emotionally and spiritually, I find that I censure what comes out of my mouth more than I did. I would say things in a joking manner, but they always had vindictive overtones. My mind still works as quickly, and the sarcastic remarks are still immediately at my disposal; but I now find I have fewer regrets and more serenity when I choose not to use them.

Resentment is like a poison or an acid that corrodes the container in which it is stored. Most of us deny our resentments and don't let them go. Therefore, we just nurse our grudges and let them smother our spiritual lives. I have heard it said resentment is like drinking poison and waiting for someone else to die.

I am learning if I admit my resentments to GOD and another person and pray that the person I resent will be granted health, happiness, and all the other things I would like for myself, then it is IMPOSSIBLE for me to harbor a resentment. At first, it is very hard to pray for someone we resent. We don't want to do it, and we certainly don't mean it; but every time we do it, we show we are willing to obey GOD and things begin to change. Before we realize it, our feeling of resentment is changed to a genuine realization that everyone has problems; no one is perfect; and our SERENITY is much more preferable to "being right"!

© 2003 Gay S. Poe

RESENTMENT

What do you do when you're really hurt
And anger and resentments are strong?

Something that's vicious – you didn't deserve;
Something so senseless – no purpose to serve.

Resentment, like poison, you can always predict
If you don't get it out, it will soon make you sick.

After the struggle, on my knees, I would pray,
"Please GOD, make me willing to give anger away."

I pray for the person who hurt me, you see,
Asking GOD that HE give him what I want for me.

The poison resentment is all drained away –
Refilled by GOD'S FREEDOM in my heart to stay.

Counting my blessings makes resentments soon flee –
Like that person is SICK and GOD takes care of me.

DON'T BARGAIN WITH GOD

*B*efore I knew much about spirituality, I had a concept of God that included a rigid program of punishment and reward. I thought if I did what God wanted me to do, then I would be rewarded for being "a good girl" and I would be punished if I had been "a bad girl." Even though I had always been told that GOD IS LOVE, I still felt there was immediate retribution for anything bad I did.

I was so misinformed that I actually believed I could make "deals" with God. Since then I have learned this is a total fallacy. In the first place, GOD DOES NOT MAKE DEALS! In the second place, I NEVER KEPT MY PART OF THE DEAL ANYWAY; and in the third place, IF NEITHER OF US PARTICIPATED, THERE COULD HAVE BEEN NO DEAL!

I used to try over and over to bargain with God. When it came time to follow through with my part of the deal, I always reneged and said, "Just one more time, God; and then I'll do my part." I really meant it each time I said it, but I could never live up to my part.

Now I have enough faith to simply ask God to give me "what I need" and know He will do it without me insulting HIM with my childish deals. I feel much more honest now that I don't always feel I have welched on a deal and lied to God.

DON'T BARGAIN WITH GOD

As I look in the mirror, I ponder and say,
"My life is a mess. Things aren't going my way."

In my Bible I've read what God can do.
I'll give it a test to see if it is true.

I'll make God a bargain: I will be good
If HE will help me and do what HE should!

I try and I try, but things just get worse.
Instead of a blessing, God's sending a curse.

Why would God do this? He's supposed to be kind.
HE won't keep His bargain – though I've tried to keep mine.

Then all of a sudden, God helps me to see.
HE doesn't make bargains – NOT EVEN WITH ME!

God surely will bless us, stay right by our side
If we yield our lives and conquer our pride.

If we give ultimatums, God won't hear our call.
He'll turn a deaf ear 'til we surrender our all.

If God needed help from you or from me,
We'd be buying salvation – God's gift that is free.

So forget all your bargains, ultimatums, and such.
Then you can relax and not worry so much.

WHO NEEDS TO CHANGE?

God grant me the serenity
To accept the things I cannot change,
Courage to change the things I can,
And wisdom to know the difference.

– *Dr. Reinhold Niebuhr*

I honestly thought this meant to use all my power along with my devious tools – such as anger, guilt, and manipulation – to get the people and situations around me, that I didn't like, to change. Then after I had exhausted all my efforts and failed, I thought I must learn to accept them. This acceptance was only to come after I had used all of my COURAGE to accomplish the change first.

The WISDOM TO KNOW THE DIFFERENCE meant I know exactly when I have failed and when to give up trying. Like any good martyr, I should think of myself and present the impression to those around me that I was a long-suffering victim of injustice.

Through many people, God finally has helped me to realize that the only things I can change are about my attitude and myself. The things about myself I don't like can be changed only as the result of my recognition of my character defects; acknowledging them to God, myself, and another human being; and humbly asking God to remove these defects. If we honestly want these defects to be removed, God will remove them in HIS TIME FRAME, not ours.

The struggle is in knowing what we can do to change ourselves and what only God can change. God's timetable is different than mine. Only when I stop fighting change and admit defeat does God give me victory over my defects, so I can be more useful for Him and enjoy a much happier life with unimaginable freedom.

This poem is about this 180-degree change in my thinking. The freedom I mentioned was in the realization that I am responsible only for my own personal change, happiness, and actions and that God is in charge of everyone else. We find we have much more energy and time to devote to God and our fellows if we do not waste it trying to control all of the people and situations around us.

God will take care of me and all those I care about – even people I don't know – if I will stay out of HIS WAY. He will take care of it anyway, but I am not nearly as bruised and bloody when I don't meddle where I don't belong.

WHO NEEDS TO CHANGE?

I used to think the "courage to change" –
When I said the Serenity Prayer –
Meant I should use all of my power
To change people and things everywhere.

I felt if they could ever see
The mistakes I saw them making,
They would mend their erring ways.
Wise counsel like mine they'd be taking.

They never seemed to realize –
When their methods they wanted to test –
That if they would only listen to me
Things would turn out for the best.

They never seemed to "thank me"
For the many hours I would spend,
Trying to arrange their lives.
Don't they know that I'm their "friend"?

Then one day I took a look
At the person I call "ME,"

And God gave me some insight
To the person others see.

My life was just a big, ole mess;
I can't take care of me.
In spite of good intentions,
I'm not all that I should be.

If I don't know what's good or bad
For me and my own life,
How could I presume to know
What will help you with your strife?

So I'll just be much better off
If I don't figure I know best
And if I don't try to give advice
But seek God's guidance like the rest.

If I can learn to just accept
The things life sends my way,
Then maybe – with God's help –
I can be happy every day.

Then I will know that "courage"
For what it's meant to be –
That I can't change the others.
THE CHANGE MUST BE IN ME!

GOD DON'T MAKE NO JUNK

A dear friend of mine was in a treatment center for alcoholism. He was very ashamed and had very low self-esteem. He felt very guilty for the harm his addiction had done to himself and others who cared about him. He felt he had sunk so low from his disease that he was unlovable and unworthy of anyone's assistance – especially GOD'S.

He could not love or forgive himself and was convinced he was unworthy of forgiveness from anyone. He said he felt like a pile of garbage. I tried to explain to him only when we get to this stage can we truly be helped. Even though I knew how much he was suffering, in my heart I knew only now could he receive GOD'S help and I felt he had taken a giant step.

As I listened to him talk and thought about what he was feeling, I remembered a little saying I read on a trinket at a craft show. I thought if I incorporated it into a poem, then it might cheer him up.

GOD DON'T MAKE NO JUNK

I woke up this morning
And considered my worth.
I'm sure I'm the most worthless
Person on earth.

I can fool other people.
I'm sure they don't see
The terrible person
I feel me to be.

My loved ones and friends
Have forgiven past deeds.
They realize I'm sick
With my own special needs.

If GOD can forgive us,
Just who are we
To punish ourselves.
ARE WE WISER THAN HE?

A little child said it –
And it's surely not "bunk":
"I'm something special!
GOD DON'T MAKE NO JUNK!"

EYES

"*The* eyes are the windows of the soul." Personally, I believe this to be a very true statement. For some, it is easy to lie with their lips, body language, etc.; but with the exception of a few sociopaths who have no conscience, it is very difficult to lie without it showing in your eyes.

I have never been a very good liar. That is not to say I never lied; but most of the time, I usually believed what I was saying to be true. This makes it easier to pull it off. The person I usually lie to (not as frequently more recently) and am the most dishonest with is myself.

In my experience, I have found I am much more open and trusting with someone who will look me straight in the eye when we are talking. I detest talking with people who are wearing dark glasses. It seems as if I am at a distinct disadvantage because their "windows" are hidden.

Most of the time, I am a fairly good judge of character and I haven't misjudged many people. Looking squarely into a person's eyes makes most of my judgments.

EYES

Can you read someone's eyes? It can be quite a curse,
For you can see right into the soul!
You can see the pain and the loneliness there –
No matter what lies you are told.

Eyes are the vulnerable part of the face;
They let you look over the wall.
They give insight as to what the truth is
And deny lies – no matter how small.

Eyes sparkle with happiness when all is well;
They sadden when burdened with care.
They tell all the secrets you try hard to hide
And say things that your mouth wouldn't dare!

I don't trust a person who looks away
When he is talking with me
'Cause I feel there's something way down deep
He'd rather that I didn't see.

So when dealing with me – if you want me to think
That you are honest and wise,
Be sure when you speak and swear it's the truth
That your MOUTH says the same as your EYES!

A SILLY SPAT

*B*efore I gained a degree of spirituality, it was very important for me to feel I was always "right." I fought valiantly not to give the impression this was the case, but inside I was very resentful that someone would disagree with me. The more they disagreed, the more gracious and manipulative I would become to win them over.

I had a very close friend, who has since passed away, who was one of the few people who had the nerve to tell this "sweet, little gray-haired lady" that some of my opinions and actions were childish and unreasonable (whether I wanted to hear it or not). One day we had a real shouting match and said many things we didn't mean, and our conversation ended on a very vindictive and sour note.

Sometimes God speaks to me in strange ways; and occasionally, it is in the form of a dream. His message was very clear, and I had absolutely no doubt as to its meaning. This revelation inspired this poem. Now I realize that being right is not nearly as important as the love between good friends.

A SILLY SPAT

One day I had a silly spat
With a friend I really love.
We've shared so many happy times;
He was a gift from up above.

He said some unkind things to me
That hurt me and I cried.
My response was sharp and harsh
To save my silly pride.

Days went by, and we didn't speak.
The rift between us grew.

Who was right or who was wrong
We never really knew.

He wouldn't give; he's too "macho."
He'd show me who was boss.
I was just as stubborn.
His WIN would be his LOSS.

Then one day someone dropped by –
Just passing by to say,
"You know that old friend you had.
I heard he died today."

I cried and mourned and grieved so much
I felt my heart would break.
When to my very great surprise,
My alarm jarred me awake.

I realized it had been a dream;
I could still make amends!
I hardly took the time to dress
To go and find my friend.

He saw me and I saw him.
We didn't say a word.
With just a hug, we understood.
Only "love" our two hearts heard.

Thank You, dear Lord, for a second chance
To be honest and be real
And tell my friend I love so much
The way I really feel.

Lives seem long, but they are short.
Swiftly, precious days go by.
Don't mar them with some silly spat
We can avoid if we just try.

APOLOGY TO MY CHILD

*F*or many years, I took it personally when one of my children would do something that seemed totally dumb or against some intrinsic value I felt I had instilled in them. I would never rant and rave and say, "Oh, how could you do this to me?" I did not blatantly say this because I was controlled by guilt trips a lot while I was growing up. I swore I would never do that to my children when I became a parent.

What I have since realized is that I did the same thing without being so obvious. Even though I did not rant and whine, it was very apparent when I was displeased or disappointed. I could accomplish with a sigh and a sad look – without saying a word – the same things my mother did by stating her feelings verbosely.

As usual, I cannot remember which child was involved in this case; but at one time or the other, it happened with all of them. One day as I sat feeling sad, let down, and guilty because my children were not absolutely perfect, I began to get a DIVINE message that shook me and said, "Do you know how much you and your children are alike?" I suddenly realized how the minor disappointments in my children could not compare to the way, as GOD'S CHILD, I had disappointed HIM. Just as I was feeling about my children, I am certain GOD feels the same about HIS CHILDREN and HE must wonder if I am worth all the bother that I cause.

As I sat and thought about this situation, GOD gave me that unspeakable assurance that makes me realize again that HE accepts us right where we are – no matter how sad we make HIM. HIS LOVE IS UNCONDITIONAL! After considering HIS PERFECT EXAMPLE, I knew, as an earthly parent, my duty is to strive to give that same kind of unconditional love to my children. I apologize to all my friends and children from whom I expect perfection – especially when GOD continues to love me in spite of the many imperfections in my own actions and attitudes.

APOLOGY TO MY CHILD

I have a child whom I felt let me down;
So I walked around with a sad, sour frown.
He seemed so self-centered, never giving a thought
To the times I had helped him or the things that I taught.

It seemed all his values were all out of place.
Guess I never noticed his tired, weary face.
I love him so much I expect him to be
Wise and unselfish and PERFECT – LIKE ME?

GOD spoke and HE said, "I know how you feel.
This being a parent is an awful tough deal.
How many times have YOU let me down?
You just stomped all My feelings right in the ground.

"You are so full of fight. You must always know
If you approve how I'm running the show.
I do not always agree with things that you do;
But with all your mistakes, I ALWAYS LOVE YOU!

"I know when you are wrong, but I never intrude.
I sit back and wait 'cause to 'butt in' is rude.
When you need My help, just call any day;
For if you don't want it, it won't help anyway.

"So back off, My child, and let your child be.
Perhaps without you, he might turn to ME.
Who better than I to know how frustration feels?
Your child or MY CHILD – it is one of those deals.

"But if you really love him, just pray for his pain
And 'butt out.' You only add to the strain.
And remember each time he disappoints you
I can name many times that you've done it too!"

THOUGHTLESS PAIN

I t has been said that no one can hurt you unless you allow it. I'm sure this is true. However, there are people in our lives whom we are very vulnerable around because they are the people whom we love. They are the ones who we are sure love and care about us.

Not knowing what to expect from strangers or acquaintances, we tend to keep our guard up. If they say something unkind or unflattering, we can pass it off as their not understanding or really knowing us. When someone we love very much – and know they love us – says something critical, cutting, and unkind, our tender feelings are exposed and we are deeply hurt.

Most of the time these remarks are quick and sarcastic and are not premeditated. The person may be having an especially bad day and needs to vent his frustration on someone, and you just happen to be handy. No malice was intended, but the sting and hurt are just as devastating as if they had been planned.

In my case, I tend to lash out at my poor husband. He is the only one who I know truly loves me – no matter what. Even though it is terrible to admit, I feel safe speaking harshly to him because I know he will forgive me. As my spirituality grows, I have been asking GOD to take this defect away. Slowly but surely, HE is answering my prayer. I am beginning to realize that the people I love most and who love me the most deserve the very best side of me, not the worst.

Thank you, dear, for all the times you let me vent my frustration on you and you responded by holding me and asking, "What can I do to help my lady?" You are a special blessing and the kindest man I know – not "henpecked" but kind. I thank GOD for you every day.

THOUGHTLESS PAIN

Have you ever noticed – and isn't it queer –
Your deepest hurts come from those you hold dear?

The people you care for and love from the start
Are the only ones able to shatter your heart!

A slight from a stranger seems fleeting and fast.
Harsh words from a loved one cause pain that will last.

Prepared for a stranger with sharp words or a frown –
With those you think love you, you let your guard down.

They surely don't realize the words that they say
Put an ache in your heart that won't go away.

They show only charm to new people they see,
While frustration and harsh words seem only for me.

I am sure I'm as guilty as they are of this sin.
LORD, help me remember as I start to again:

Understanding and kind words – about which we may boast –
Should be shared with the people WHO LOVE US THE MOST!

IN THE NAME OF LOVE

*T*he role of a parent is one of the most exasperating – yet one of the most rewarding – in the world. We have absolutely no prior preparation for it; and most of the time, we feel totally inadequate.

As is the case with most parents, we wanted our children to have all of the things we never had – as well as anything they wanted. This goal had to be accomplished – no matter what sacrifices were involved by their father and me.

You may have heard the story of how a baby chick that is not allowed to break out of the shell on its own will not be strong enough to survive. In my overzealous attempt to protect my children from the hard knocks of life, I have broken many "egg shells."

In HIS infinite MERCY, I feel GOD rewarded my good intentions and helped my children to become useful, loving, caring, and responsible citizens in spite of my well-meaning mistakes. All of these mistakes were made in the name of love.

I was sincere, but I was sincerely WRONG! Thank You, LORD, for giving my children and me what we needed and not what we thought we needed.

IN THE NAME OF LOVE

Do you want your children to have
All the things you never had?
Do you sacrifice (often too much)
To protect them from life when it's bad?

Do you shield them from things they need to learn
Because they might be unhappy and cry?
Do you torture yourself needlessly
About each new, little thing they must try?

Do you make life too easy and hide the real truth
'Bout the real lives we live every day?
Do we unknowingly lie and let them believe
They can avoid obstacles put in their way?

Do we hand them for free the things they should earn?
Do we make them shallow and weak?
Do we thwart GOD'S lesson that says,
"You must work for whatever you seek"?

The mistakes we make in the name of love
Make them soft and they learn to depend.
Teaching these lies we constantly sell
Is disservice, not being their friend.

Real love teaches truth (hard though it may be)
And helps if one needs a hand.
Selfish love robs another of growth,
And he never learns how to stand.

So when they grow up and cannot cope,
We criticize and we frown;
But how could they know "how far it was
If they were carried each step into town."

MASTER PLAN

*W*hen my younger son was sixteen years old, he was involved in an automobile accident in which one of the young boys in the vehicle was killed. Death was instantaneous. He was thrown through the rear window.

It was such a seemingly senseless tragedy. All of the parents and the young people (there were four boys in the vehicle) had a very difficult time accepting what had happened. We all wanted an answer to the age-old question: "WHY?"

As usual, when I seek GOD, HE reveals things to me and helps me process events I don't understand. I still don't usually understand, but HE lets me accept the situation and gives me a peace with which I can live.

This peace comes from the realization that GOD is in charge and has a MASTER PLAN. It is like the underside of a tapestry that makes no sense from that perspective, but GOD sees the other side where a wonderful plan and design are unfolding.

I wrote this poem for my son to help him understand that his life was spared as part of GOD'S GREAT MASTER PLAN. Therefore, he should be grateful and attempt – with GOD'S HELP – to be and accomplish what GOD has planned for his life.

MASTER PLAN

Tragedy strikes and everything changes.
In a matter of moments, your life rearranges.
A young boy is gone – the same age as my son.
We don't understand why he was the one.

One moment so carefree, savoring life,
Too young to have known real worry or strife.
The next moment death, with its terrible sting,
Had snuffed out his life, such a beautiful thing.

Four lives in the balance; only one life was taken.
The others were only cut, bruised, and shaken.
Gratitude and relief that it was not my son –
From the look of the truck, he should be the one

That GOD took that night when they hit the pole
'Cause he did the driving – as the story is told.
GOD spared his life for a reason I know.
In GOD'S TIME, He will prove and will show

That his life was worth saving and He'll use it well
To serve GOD and live life; so other people can tell.
GOD made a good choice by letting him live
For the contribution his spared life can give.

GOD, don't let him waste it or throw it away;
But give it to YOU with each bright, new day.
Even though he's still young, let him understand
His life is a part of YOUR MASTER PLAN!

LORD, I'M SO TIRED

*W*hen I remember all of the blessings I have, it makes me so ashamed. I have never had much patience with people who complain and whine about something all the time. However, some days I feel myself becoming one of those people; and it repulses me. I have often asked my doctor, "Why couldn't this be happening to someone who would enjoy the doctors, the attention, and the fact they are disabled?" I have always thought God has a terrific sense of humor to put my five-year-old mentality into this beaten-up, old body.

I grieve over the things I cannot do any longer, but I rejoice in the things I can STILL do. I would be happier if I could be climbing trees and going down slides at the park; but I try to remember I am blessed with beautiful, healthy, happy grandchildren who seem to love me anyway.

I have grown spiritually because of all my physical problems, for they have forced me to be still and listen to what God has to tell me. These problems have made it possible for me to experience the feelings in my poetry, and they have taught me there are ways to be helpful – even with my problems – rather than helpless because of them.

I am not going to lie and say this is the path I would have chosen if I had chosen, but God has a plan and I know that is what is important. I pray when I am gone that I will be remembered for my sense of humor in the midst of adversity and for my HELPFULNESS rather than my HELPLESSNESS. Thank YOU for all the people who help me bear the pain!

LORD, I'M SO TIRED

Oh Lord, I'm so tired.
My body's in pain.
I have problems in my life
That torture my brain.

I've tried so hard, Lord.
Please help me to find
A Godly solution
To have peace of mind.

When the problem is me, Lord,
'Cause I try to be YOU,
Please give me a sign
What YOU want me to do.

I don't mean to complain
'Cause YOU give so much.
I'm only asking
For Your healing touch.

Put my life back together,
And clean out my soul.
Spread on Your balm
That will make my life whole.

Please help me remember
That when I moan and whine
I'm no use to You
And Your glory can't shine!

Please make what YOU need
From this life I've been given.
Take away the self-pity.
Help me get on with livin'!

ALL IN THE DOOR

*H*aving grown a great deal in the spiritual realm in the last few years, I have found the faith necessary to believe that GOD has a plan for me – as well as for each of my children. HIS PLAN will be executed – no matter what I choose to do.

This faith was a long time in coming, and I wasted many needless hours on worry and sleeplessness. I also received a head full of white hair in the process.

I always felt it part of my duty as a mother to pace, worry, protect, and manage my children's lives. I felt responsible for their behavior – both good and bad. I was definitely responsible for their happiness – or the lack thereof. It was an awesome and exhausting task.

I embraced this illusion of control. It kept me anxious and upset. This situation made me feel like a juggler in the circus that had to keep all the balls in the air without dropping one. It seemed if one child or person for whom I felt responsible was doing well, then two others were out of place.

After I gave up the struggle, it became clear that GOD is in charge of everything. HIS PLAN will prevail – whether we walk the floor and worry or we simply quit this job we cannot possibly handle.

I began to pray and turn everyone over to GOD. HE knows what each one needs, and HE loves them more than I do. HE only wants good things for them; and unlike me, HE knows what these things are. Whether we walk the floor or go to bed and get our rest so we can be more effective parents or friends, the next day things still turn out the same.

A wise man once said, "Worry is like a rocking chair. It gives you something to do while you wait." A friend of mine tells me: "Worrying insults GOD." This poem is a "Mother's Lament" and illustrates how agonizing parenting can be without faith.

ALL IN THE DOOR

From the moment they're born – if you want the facts,
You worry and fret and never relax.

When they are infants, you sleep with one eye –
Afraid if they need you, you won't hear their cry.

Bruises and bumps and pets that are lost,
You try hard to soothe them – whatever the cost.

Problems with homework and sports that are played –
In spite of their bad teams and weather, you stayed.

When they were sick, you stayed by their bed,
Praying and wishing it could be you instead.

When they were older, the affairs of the heart –
This will be harder, you know from the start.

Learning to drive – they start to date.
This is so hard; you must learn to wait.

They should be home; your heart pounds with fright.
Ten minutes seem hours when you're waiting at night.

Finally, a car door – your heart skips a beat –
Only to realize the car's 'cross the street.

It seems like forever; your long vigil ends.
"Hi, Mom, did you worry? We were out with our friends."

"Thank You, dear GOD" – as I kneel on the floor.
"I can't get my rest 'til they're all in the door."

Years pass so quickly; the cycle goes on.
I just turn around, and it seems they are grown.

Their problems are theirs now; I can't bear their pain.
I wish I could spare them, but I'm wishing in vain.

When I get to heaven, I know there's a door
Where millions of mothers have waited before.

They stray from the path; the darkness will fall.
"Please, GOD, bring them back. Let them hear YOUR call.

"I know Your promise. YOUR BOOK tells me so:
'Just train up a child in the way he should go.'

"I've made mistakes, Father; but I did my best.
I've done all I can; YOU must do the rest.

"Praise GOD!" They are coming; I hear the glad sound.
I see their sweet faces; they won't let us down.

It seemed like forever, but night turns to day.
"Hi, Mom! Did you worry? You showed us the way.

"Thank YOU, DEAR FATHER," I've said it before.
"I can't get my rest 'til they're all in the door!"

WITH LOVE TO OUR KIDS

J have had the good fortune to be involved with many teenagers in my life, and I love them. I get so frustrated and saddened when I hear people moaning and complaining about their teenagers and their noisy friends.

The teenage years of my children and their friends were some of the most favorite times of my life. They included me in all of their antics, and we had a ball.

Our home was always, during their growing-up years, the one with the baseball diamond worn out in the front lawn, the one with the screen door on the carport entrance ripped or torn out altogether from street hockey pucks, and the one with bicycle ramps all over. I never told them "no" to most anything they wanted to do – unless it was illegal or too totally dangerous. For this reason, they knew when "Mama Gay" said "NO," I had a very good reason and it was usually respected.

One particular night, they wanted to go someplace that I felt was dangerous because of some racial unrest in the area. I gave them an emphatic "NO" when they told me where they wanted to go. After awhile, they left, saying they were going somewhere else. I knew exactly where they were going, but I didn't stop them. I said, "Okay" and I waited. My son and daughter came back almost immediately, and the others dribbled back in one by one. The whole group was back within thirty minutes. One of my son's friends said, "I don't know why, but I can't lie to you. It is easy to lie to my parents. They say, 'NO' automatically without even thinking about it; but I know YOU trust us!" For this fabulous compliment and all of the enjoyment they gave me, this poem is dedicated to some of my favorite people –TEENAGERS!

WITH LOVE TO OUR KIDS

I get so tired of hearing folks say,
"Teenagers are rotten and selfish today!"

When adults show distrust – lashing verbal abuse,
It makes a kid think, "I can't win! What's the use?"

When he's shown indifference and self-centered ways,
He'll give it right back the rest of his days.

Young lives are like mirrors; they only reflect
The things that they see. Why not love and respect?

If adults take the time to instill self-esteem,
A child can be anything – whatever his dream.

Kids can live without money. They all learn to share;
But they cannot survive without someone to care.

They talk if we listen; they respond to a touch.
At this stage of life, they need it so much.

They have lots of fun without smoking or drinking.
Proud of their bodies, they're wise in their thinking.

Through happy and sad times, they all stick together –
True friends to the end – whatever the weather.

When a child has a parent on whom to depend,
He'll make them proud and he'll be their friend.

If you don't want to rile me, you'd better not say,
"Teenagers really are rotten today"

Because I'll know in an instant – it really will show –
You don't know the same ones I'VE BEEN BLESSED TO KNOW!

WHATEVER JUDGMENT

*O*ne day I had the unfortunate experience of being caught up in an encounter – very loud and very verbally abusive – between a dear friend of mine and his young son. The son had pulled one of the "bonehead" pranks so common to adolescents; and to say his dad was perturbed would be a vast understatement.

The youngster seemed to always be in trouble of some kind or the other. He was not a bad kid; but if he were in a group of fifty kids that pulled a prank, he is the one who would always be caught.

My friend had lost all patience and spoke to his son very harshly. I watched the young boy and saw him flinch with every unkind word, and his pain touched my heart.

God gave me this poem as a result of that incident. It reminded me that the Bible says, "With whatsoever judgment you judge, so shall you be judged." As I reflected on the incident, I thanked God that HE gives us "MERCY" and not "JUSTICE."

WHATEVER JUDGMENT

It's so easy to say what another should do
In situations another is facing.
Our patience is short, criticism is harsh
When someone else the devil is pacing.

We get all self-righteous; our confidence soars.
It's so simple what they should have done.
But stand back and think when the problem was yours,
Were YOU wise and confident, Son?

With whatever judgment you render, my friend,
This one thing God says to believe.
"Harshness or mercy is yours to decide,
But BE CAREFUL! The same you'll receive."

'Cause we all make mistakes – except for our Lord
In whose judgment our futures all rest.
So search your own heart before you decide:
"How might I have handled HIS test?"

For our God is love and so must we be
If His image we wish to reflect.
So offer a hand, not a sharp reprimand;
And you'll earn the Father's respect!

ENGAGE BRAIN BEFORE PUTTING MOUTH IN MOTION

*W*hen I was a child, I was often told: "Words are like arrows shot into the air. Once they are released, they can never be retrieved." Gossip, which is character assassination in its vilest form – as well as unkind words spoken without thought – definitely fall into this category.

Before I gained a degree of spirituality and maturity, it was always my modus operandi to react rather than think and act later. I was very selective about whom I got angry with because I only vented on people who I knew loved me and would forgive my ridiculous outbursts.

Slowly I am learning to vent my anger in healthier ways. I talk it out with an objective person or persons who are not involved or cannot be hurt by the situation. Then I ask God to remove my anger – and any fear that was at the root of my anger – in order for me to sanely assess the situation. I either set boundaries with the object of my anger or let it go with no action because it wasn't that important anyway.

Sometimes I suffer from "selective amnesia" and resort to my old tactics but not nearly as frequently as I used to do. Now on most occasions, I remember that anger – even justified anger – is a luxury I cannot afford and is certainly too high a price to pay for my "serenity"!

ENGAGE BRAIN BEFORE PUTTING MOUTH IN MOTION

I let my temper get out of control.
Temporarily, I was insane.
It was only after I really went wild
That my anger started to wane.

I said terrible things that hurt one I love –
Harsh words that were vulgar and mean.
And try as I might when I close my eyes,
I relive this terrible scene.

The one that I hurt quickly forgave,
And I also ask God to forgive;
But in spite of all I know in my heart,
These unpleasant words will still live.

I learned a lesson that I'd never known,
And I think I'll remember forever:
Words once spoken can't be retrieved;
So from now on, I'm sure I'll endeavor,-

When angry again, I'll try to think first
'Bout my words – whatever my notion –
And try to be sure my brain is in gear
'Fore I put my big mouth in motion!

ONE MORE TALK

*W*hen you lose someone you love with whom you have a very close personal relationship, there is a deep loneliness inside you. This deep well of loneliness can be drained only by GOD'S COMFORT and the "balm" of time. Grieving and healing are processes we must go through. The longer we try to deny our grief, the longer the process takes.

Even when this special person was ill for years and you knew death was inevitable, even though we had discussed our feelings for each other on many occasions, there is still that longing for one more talk. Being human – even if this wish could be granted, it would not be enough. It is our nature that we always want more.

In one case, I had twelve years to prepare myself for the inevitable loss I knew was in store for me; but still I find myself once in awhile wishing for just "one more talk." Sometimes I fantasize about this imaginary talk and what I would say if I had the chance.

ONE MORE TALK

When someone you love
Is taken away,
There are so many things
You wish you could say.

If we could talk by the fire
Just one more sweet time
And I could just hold
His big hand in mine.

He knew that I loved him –
There wasn't a doubt.
I told him so often
Sometimes he would shout:

"You've shown me your love
In so many ways;
And as far as for saying it,
You've missed very few days!"

I'd like to thank him
For the things that he taught
And the wisdom he shared –
Though we always fought.

I'd tell him I miss him
Each single day –
That he's burned in my heart
In his own special way.

I'd ask for forgiveness
For mistakes that I made,
For now I can see
Many times that he paid.

Then I'd assure him
I'd never forget
A day that we spent
From the day that we met.

I'd make him understand –
Though I feel so much pain –
I wouldn't have missed it;
I'd do it again.

I'd thank him for loving me
When I was sick and afraid,
Let him know what that meant –
The difference it made.

I'd want one more "bear hug"
With all the strength that it gave
To lock in my heart
Forever to save.

Reluctantly, I'd let him go,
My very special friend –
But only if he'd promise
That we would meet again.

HERE I AM AGAIN, LORD

*I*t has been revealed to me that to attain God's will in my life I must not only ask for it but I must "BE STILL" and free my mind, so I can hear God speaking to me. It isn't that God cannot speak to me through any amount of clamor, noise, and other distractions because He has. Yet, like myself, He prefers to speak quietly to an interested, open-minded person who is giving Him his undivided attention. I go to God with the same problems and faults so often that I cannot even fathom the patience it requires to always be there for me.

Without a struggle or a fight, it seems I never learn anything and I can continue this struggle for as long as I choose. God is so polite! He gives us the choice; but when I decide I am powerless and exhausted and I am willing to BE STILL and LISTEN, GOD is always ready with the answer.

HERE I AM AGAIN, LORD!!

Here I am again, Lord,
Knocking at Your door.
I'm so tired of struggling;
I can't fight it anymore!

My mind is tired; my body's sick.
I've abused Your temple so;
But I don't have to tell You
'Cause You already know.

Fear and anger fill my days;
Self-pity rules my life.
I hate myself and others.
I'm the cause of so much strife.

Lord, let me see that I can't change

The things that others do.
Help me be strong, so I'll forgive
THE WAY YOU ALWAYS DO!

I want to be a butterfly
That's beautiful to see –
Not the ugly caterpillar
That, without You, I would be.

I can make no promises
'Cause I'm human and I'm weak.
Please teach me to be still, Lord;
So I can hear You speak.

Only You can tame my spirit
And give serenity.
I'll ask again, "YOU TAKE CONTROL"
And make the best of me.

Forgive my sins, my pride, and lies
To others and myself.
Teach me to GET RID OF THEM,
Not put them on the shelf.

And now I want to ask You, Lord,
While writing through my tears:
"Please take away some of my TONGUE,
And put it on my EARS!!!"

THERE'S NO PLACE LIKE HOME

*M*y children have always had pets of one kind or another. They ranged from goldfish to spider monkeys. My youngest son always had a cat – even though he was allergic to them. We had a variety of cats with names that ranged from "Sooty" because he was solid black to "Clorox" because she was almost paisley and looked like someone had accidentally spilled bleach on her.

The dogs were the bane of my existence because, as far as I know, there was never one that was housebroken or shouldn't have been drowned at birth. They ranged from one named "Puppy" (simple but functional) to "Jack Peter Brown" who was named after someone that was on a TV show at the time we acquired him.

"Peter Brown" was especially interesting because he came whining up to the back door with his head swollen twice the normal size on a cold and rainy New Year's Day, and I thought he had been bitten by a snake. We took him to the vet who laughed and said, "Have your children had the mumps?" They, of course, had.

We had "Buck," a white German Shepherd, that a friend bought at a bar when he was drunk. He thought he was cute at five pounds. It was quite a different story when he weighed 150 pounds, and he lived in a small apartment where pets were not allowed; so you guessed it! I got lucky!! The 'Buck' stopped here!

Maybe because I was older and more tired – and besides all my children were grown, I think the appearance of "BOOGER BEAR O'BRYANT" (you'd never guess my son is an Alabama fan) was the most distressing. He nearly drove me nuts. He drooled, dragged, and chewed on everything I owned and barked constantly. Just before all my neighbors got up a petition to have us all removed from the neighborhood, God took pity on me and he moved away. Ecstatic is the word that comes to mind. My happiness and sense of relief could be compared only to the way a young bride feels as her new in-laws drive away after an unannounced visit. I love well-behaved animals like I love well-behaved children, but even then it is so much more pleasant an experience when they are not mine.

THE HEALING BED

THERE'S NO PLACE LIKE HOME WHEN IT AIN'T MINE

"Booger O'Bryant" is a fine Irish Setter.
As most setters go, he couldn't be better.

He came to my house with his proud, handsome "father"
Who said, "Isn't he cute? He won't be any bother!"

He was doing O.K. 'til one day he knew
That he had some teeth and he started to chew.

Ten pairs of shoes; and in spite of my wrath,
He ate anything that got in his path.

"He's just a puppy," his "father" would say.
"He'll start to calm down most any day."

We put him outside. What things could he do?
Believe me, my friend, he found quite a few.

He first ate a table and all of the chairs –
only the start of my miseries and cares.

He dug holes in the yard. You could bury a cow!
Georgia clay so hard, no farmer could plow!

He scraped muddy claws on the sliding glass doors.
My screams and my threats he promptly ignored.

He barks all the time 'til the neighbors all call,
But the drooling red idiot's having a ball.

Four times my white drapes he dragged to the yard –
$16.50 a cleaning. That dog's really a card.

His "dad" bought a house without any fence.
I can't say I blame him. He was using good sense.

'Bout my birthday gifts – no words did I mince:
"What I want most for you, my dear, is a fence!"

He built a fence; and as he took him away,
I shed not a tear. It made my whole day!

My advice, son, if he jumps the fence
And his actions begin to keep you in suspense

And he grabs your curtain and he starts to pull it,
Forget about fences and give him a bullet!

YOU KNOW HOW I FEEL

*T*he story was told of the time a reporter asked the mother of then President Eisenhower: "Mrs. Eisenhower, aren't you proud of your son?" She quickly replied, "Which one?" I could always relate to that story because that seemed to sum up my feelings about my children.

At another time, a wise mother was asked, "Which of your children do you love the most?" Her answer put my feelings exactly in words: "I love the one that is in trouble, the one most hurt, the one that is sickest, or the one that is having the most difficulty at the time."

There have been occasions in the lives of each of my children when an outsider might have thought I was partial to one and gave them more love and attention. However, anyone close enough to really understand the situation realized that, at one time or the other, each of my children has been the one I loved, cared for, and was partial to in their particular time of crisis.

I can't even remember which of my children I wrote this poem about; but at one time or another, it could have applied to any one of them. It is a very painful, frightening, and helpless feeling when your child is in pain – either physical or emotional; and there is nothing you can do. My old way of dealing with such a situation was to dive right into the middle of their problems and try to "FIX" them. This only perpetuated and intensified the problems.

Gratefully, I have learned that MY PART in their problems is to pray for them, asking GOD to give them what they need. I need to be supportive and available without interference. The only way I am strong enough to change my old habits of years is to be ever mindful that the children are not mine but loaned and entrusted to me by GOD. HE loves them and knows what is best for them much more than I. If I try to protect them from pain and pressure that GOD may be using to shape their lives, I will be hurt and that child will have to struggle even longer to learn the lesson GOD is trying to teach.

This lesson GOD is trying to teach will keep appearing in various forms until it is learned. Therefore, the sooner the lesson is learned, the less painful it will be. UNSELFISH LOVE "LETS GO AND LETS GOD"!

YOU KNOW HOW I FEEL

Dear LORD, my child's hurting.
I wish he could know
That I'm hurting too
Because I love him so.

Pain's not so bad
When it is my own,
But his pain hurts much worse –
Even though he is grown.

A kiss heals a young child
And calms all his fears;
But when he's an adult,
Only prayers and my tears

Are the weapons I have
To help me feel a part
Of helping to heal
My child's broken heart.

Maybe this is the way
You help me to see
The wonderful thing
That YOU did for me.

You watched YOUR SON suffer
On the cross in HIS pain
And silently listened
As HE called YOUR NAME,

So we could be saved
From our sin that HE bore
And make us a way
To reach heaven's door.

So bless my child, FATHER,
And help him to bear
All of his troubles
That I cannot share.

Help him to see
That only YOUR LOVE
Can give him that PEACE
That comes from above.

L I F E   L E S S O N S   F R O M

FLY WITH ME

*N*ature is full of object lessons that show me how to better live my life and what I may expect if I look for a miracle. Nature is full of miracles. Think of all the animals, seeds, and insects that start out so ugly; and by GOD'S WILL, they are changed into something beautiful. These changes occur easily and without a struggle because the animals and insects have not been given a choice. We, on the other hand, can obtain this change – and the happiness that comes with it – only by making a conscious choice to turn our will over to HIM and admit that only GOD can make us beautiful.

As I quit struggling and relax, I become pliable and GOD can recreate me in HIS IMAGE. As I am relieved of the stress involved in trying to be in control, I continue to get stronger, better, and more spiritually beautiful each day.

Through faith in GOD, I learn to trust. My fears fall away because I have the peace that comes only through surrender. GOD enables me to soar to heights I never dreamed possible.

"FLY WITH ME" is my attempt to describe the difference I feel when I am transformed from my hopeless, helpless, and negative state into a state of GRACE. This transition assures me that no matter what mistakes I make, I can always return to GOD and HIS WILL where there is always hope, help, and another chance if I just ask for it.

FLY WITH ME!

An ugly brown caterpillar crawled in the dust,
Aimlessly drifting – with no one to trust.

His eyes were downcast; he hated his life.
The faster he crawled, the greater his strife!

He kept plodding along day after day

With no one to tell him of a new, better way.

Then one day he heard the flutter of wings.
It made him look up – he saw wonderful things!

A beautiful butterfly flew into view:
"Don't despair, Little Friend. I once was like you!

"My life, too, was hopeless; or that's how it seemed;
But great things can happen – more than you dreamed!

"That problem you're having is not solved by will.
If you want things to change, you have to be still!

"Let that life that you hate be wrapped up in GOD'S LOVE,
And your spirit will change with help from above."

It all happened so slowly – he was hardly aware;
But all those around him saw the change that was there.

The ugly brown body was a beautiful yellow;
The once heavy spirit was happy and mellow.

The life that was earthbound is now never boring.
Changes occurred; his new spirit is soaring.

Now if he feels low or begins to look back,
He thinks of the old days and remembers the fact

That the more he lets go, the harder he'll try
To get closer to GOD; so the higher he'll fly!

Maybe once in awhile, he'll land in the dust
But knows now to look up to the ONE HE CAN TRUST.

So with faith in himself and in this new power,
This beautiful creature goes from flower to flower,

Spreading the message of what peace one can find
When there's love in his heart and GOD on his mind.

CHRISTMAS SIDE TRIP

*I*t was going to be a rather quiet Christmas for the family. My daughter and granddaughter and my new son-in-law were celebrating with his family in south Florida. That meant my husband and two sons would help make up our holiday group.

A very dear friend of ours suffered a bad heart attack when he was thirty-one years old. He was having some pain and irregular heartbeats that meant he would spend Christmas in coronary care. We were all sad about this. He was in a surly, "poor pitiful me" frame of mind and was very depressed. He definitely did not like the idea of spending Christmas Eve and Christmas in the hospital.

My health had not been good, and I had been out of the hospital for only a few days. However, my older son and I decided fairly late on Christmas Eve afternoon to go visit our friend to try to cheer him up.

After we had visited with him for awhile, he seemed to be feeling a little better; so we started for home. It had been raining, and it was getting really cold.

My son had a fairly new four-wheel drive truck, and he was very proud of it. Before my unexpected, long-term illness set in, we were notorious for pulling crazy stunts.

Because I was barely twenty when my son was born, we grew up together. He and his friends always felt I was "one of the guys," and my disability and limitations had been really hard on both of us. My involvement in some of their "shenanigans" had been curtailed, and we were both having trouble accepting that "the old grey mare wasn't what she used to be."

On the way home from the hospital, we both spotted a wooded side road that beckoned to us as the perfect place to go "four wheeling." My son looked at me and I looked at him and we both smiled knowingly. As we took the sudden turn off the main road into the woods, we both felt the adrenalin start to pump. We were both excited to be up to our old tricks.

Most of the time, the best four wheeling is done in the mud because there is more slipping and sliding and it makes the adventure more exciting. On this particular occasion, the mud – combined with the fact we were at the top of a large hill – was a tricky combination. Both of us felt that a four-wheel-drive pickup could go in and out of every situation; WE WERE WRONG! As we tried to turn around to go back to civilization, we began to slide. We slid down to a point where we were flush up against a medium-size pine tree. We were so close we could not open the driver-side door, and we knew if we tried to rock back and forth to get unstuck we would take all the paint off that side of my son's new truck.

For some stupid reason, I had chosen a pink pantsuit to wear to the hospital that day. Believe me, it was a bad choice. It had rained so much that the good old "Georgia red mud" was about six or eight inches deep all around the truck. We both took off our shoes and rolled up our pants legs and got out to survey the situation. My getting out was over the loud protests of my son saying, "You just got out of the hospital!" We tried several things but finally had to conclude that we were stuck and could do nothing on our own.

It was beginning to get dark, and we knew my husband and other son would be getting worried. We also knew they would call the hospital to ask what time we left, and that would worry our friend too! I had been hospitalized for a respiratory problem, and I knew I'd never be able to walk out of the woods. By then, it was after 8 p.m. and very dark. It was very creepy up in those woods – and especially since we had seen what looked like a marijuana patch earlier in an isolated section of the woods.

After much argument and deliberation, we finally came to the conclusion that the only answer was for my son to walk the several miles down to a convenience store we had passed. I was to wait in the truck with the doors locked.

It was Christmas Eve night. I was certain my loved ones were worried sick (little did they know we were only five or six miles from them). I was cold and hungry; and I longed to walk in our family room where there was a beautiful Christmas tree, a warm fire, and delicious food waiting for me.

My mind wandered in an attempt to take my thoughts off my present circumstances. As I looked up at the stars, I thought of Mary and Joseph and how uncomfortable they must have been on that Christmas when they traveled so far. They had to be so weary and had no place to go for warmth, food, and shelter. All that was available to them was a stable with livestock for company. There was no bright delivery room with trained personnel to assist Mary with her Son's birth and no crowned heads or lofty public officials who were excitedly expecting this miraculous birth. Like the rest of JESUS' life, His birth was humble and simple and was attended by shepherds and angels and announced by a beautiful Christmas Star that came to shine on the manger that held the CHRIST CHILD.

No Christian Dior baby clothes were available; He was wrapped in swaddling clothes. No fancy Bassett crib was available; so He lay in a manger on clean, sweet-smelling straw. As a mother, I can remember that each time I gave birth I felt I had the most wonderful baby in the world. I can only imagine the mixture of humility and pride Mary must have felt knowing she had given birth to the SON OF GOD and the SAVIOR of us all.

I don't know how long it was that my mind drifted in the star-filled night before I heard someone coming and my mind snapped back to the present. I must admit I was afraid until I realized it was my two sons and my husband coming to rescue me. Relief flooded over me, and I was even ready to take the scolding for how stupid it was to take such chances. My son had brought a bow saw, and they quickly cut down the little pine tree that was blocking our escape. In only a few minutes, we were on our way to warmth, shelter, and food. I said a "thank you" prayer for our rescue; my wonderful, loving family (who loves me unconditionally even when I do dumb things); but most of all, for my HEAVENLY FATHER who always knows where I am, what I need, and when I need it. As I walked into our home – muddy, cold, and hungry, I had a glimpse of what it would be like to get to heaven and feel the warmth and unconditional love that will be mine forever.

Am I sorry we took that side trip? Not on your life! It is a warm and fuzzy experience that none of my family will forget. As always, IT WAS A LEARNING EXPERIENCE! The area where we were that night has long since been cleared and covered with high-rise buildings; but when I pass there, I remember that night. Like Mary, I kept these things and pondered them in my heart!

THE DIAMOND

*W*hen my older son was in his early twenties, he gave me a wonderful surprise. It was a beautiful solitaire diamond on a gold chain. Parents are usually the ones doing the sacrificing; so it is a special, rewarding event to receive a thoughtful gift for no reason. I knew he had to save and sacrifice for it, and I was very touched.

I was ecstatic over the beautiful and unexpected gift that my son gave me because he wanted to give me a "love gift." I was, however, even more ecstatic for the reason and sentiment involved in me receiving it. That was the "real gift," and it is locked forever in the part of my heart where I store special things.

"Diamonds may be a girl's best friend"; but a compliment or a gesture of thoughtfulness, love, and respect are a mother's "most valued possession." Whether it is the first dandelion (to which you are probably allergic) your child brings you or a $5-million-dollar mansion, the message is the same: "I love you, Mom" – the sweetest words a mother can hear.

THE DIAMOND

My son gave me a diamond;
It cost him quite a lot.

It made me very happy
To see the thrill he got

By knowing he had pleased me
And made me feel so good.

He knew inside that I would cry;
I reacted – as I should.

It really made me very proud
To know he cared so much –

Even though he says he loves me
Every day with word or touch.

It was really not the diamond
That set my heart aglow.

It was what he said that warmed my heart –
He might not even know.

He held my hand and said to me
At our conversation's end:

"It's great that you're my mother;
But even greater, you're my friend."

EASIER GETTING IN THAN GETTING OUT

 ne cool fall morning, I went out on the deck of our house which backs up to ten acres of wooded land.

I sat clearing my head with a cup of coffee and trying to "be still and know that God is God" and asking for the knowledge of His will for my day.

Thankfully, I have reached the point where I know if I ask God to speak to me He will. God uses many ways. It may be through another person, a sunrise or sunset, a child's behavior, an animal, etc.; but I always receive a message if I am open minded and willing to be still and listen. This particular morning God used a squirrel as my object lesson and, thus, the following poem.

EASIER GETTING IN THAN OUT

Early this morning
I saw a strange sight –
One of God's creatures
Caught up in a fight.

A big, fat gray squirrel,
Who was happy and free,
Had to go in a place
Where he shouldn't be.

He struggled and fought,
Crawling in a small hole.
One little acorn –
That was his goal.

As one of God's creatures,
I'm sure that he knew
That hole was too small
And he shouldn't go through.

Well, he couldn't get out.
He knew he was caught,
And he wished he'd remembered
All the things he'd been taught.

I watched him struggle.
I could see his fur swell.
His eyes showed his fear.
I could see them and tell.

He finally gave up
And sat rather calm.
I almost could sense
A heavenly balm

That covered his body
And let him slide free,
And I had to laugh –
He was so much like me!

That acorn he wanted
That caused all the mess
Fell back in the birdhouse,
And he couldn't care less.

I, too, get in trouble
When I think I need more;
And God says,
"Stay out. I'm closing this door."

But I struggle to get in,
And sometimes I do;
But I'm in real trouble
That always is true.

My Heavenly Father
Just lets me squirm -
In hopes that perhaps
Ole Stubborn might learn.

If He tells me:
"NO! YOU'VE GOT ENOUGH!"
And I disagree
And try to get tough,

Then I'm gonna pay
For having my way;
But just for the record,
I'd like to say,

"Trouble is easy
To get into no doubt;
But it truly is hell
'Til God helps me out!"

GOD'S SNOW

*T*here is nothing quite as beautiful to me as the landscape after a beautiful snowfall of several inches. Everything is so clean and pure. It looks as though God has covered all the ugliness and clutter of the world with a clean, white fresh surface to let us see how perfect we – as well as the world could be – if we just let God have His way in our lives.

This morning when I awoke to this fresh snowfall, I had a spiritual experience that changed my outlook on my whole day. God's signature is everywhere every day – if we just look for it; but some days we feel God signs so magnificently that we can't possibly miss it – even with our finite minds. This poem is about such a day.

GOD'S SNOW

I woke up this morning with aches and pains
And started my day with disgust.
I didn't take time to thank God at all
Or remember He deserves all my trust.

As I staggered, half blind, to my coffee cup,
My eyes caught a beautiful sight.
It had started to snow, which is very rare,
And I perked up with childish delight.

Millions of snowflakes floated to earth.
I remembered what once I had read:
Each one is different; no two are the same.
"Not even snowflakes," God said.

If He took the time to fashion each flake –
As short as its lifetime would be,
Imagine the love and effort He spent
To create a person like me!

The ground that was marred with careless debris
Became a beautiful, breathtaking white.
What once was so ugly that you turned away
Was a pure and wonderful sight.

As I watched with wonder this marvelous change,
I remembered what God did for me –
How His gentle love covered my sins
And made me a fit sight to see!

The earth, when the snow melts, still shows the stains
That were covered up for awhile;
But my stains can't come back. God took them away.
He forgets them, for that is His style.

How can I take a wonderful, bright new day
That God has given to me
And waste its promise – without even a thought
Of what HE meant it to be???

God's people, like snowflakes, should cover the earth
And give it new beauty each day;
So others can see what God can do
And know that HE IS THE WAY!!!

THE CHOICE

*B*ecause of medication I took when I was pregnant with my only daughter, she was diagnosed with cancer when she was only nineteen years of age. They tried several procedures to avoid a hysterectomy, but the drug had caused so many abnormalities in her reproductive system that the doctor decided a hysterectomy was the safest course of action. She was by now twenty years old.

Even though I was only nineteen when the drug was prescribed for me in good faith to prevent a miscarriage, I was still riddled with guilt. In my "magic, magnifying mind," I felt I was totally responsible. I cried secretly and sometimes even openly. My daughter did not blame me. However, I carried around enough guilt for both of us.

All of her life, my daughter had one goal; and that was to marry and have LOTS of children. Between my guilt and her feeling so cheated, we were a pitiful pair.

GOD – in HIS GOODNESS, seeing how much we all needed a baby, saw fit to give us one. She was beautiful, perfect, and our own little "MIRACLE." She was four days old when we brought her home. She tipped the scale at an even four pounds and was fifteen inches long. Secretly, I worried she might be a midget; but we didn't care! We dressed her in doll clothes (honestly), and she wore "preemie" diapers.

That was twenty years ago; and she is still beautiful, intelligent, and loving. She is still our special "miracle." She is loved as much or more than any child has ever been.

I thank GOD every day for her and her birth mother. The BIRTH MOTHER was a teenager with no support system, and she understood she had no way to care for her. I am so grateful to this young mother that she did not choose to do away with this beautiful baby we love so much. This poem is dedicated to all the brave mothers who choose life rather than destruction.

THE CHOICE

This shouldn't have happened – a moment's mistake,
A life in my body to give or to take.

Many choices are open – or so people say,
But most feel that I should just wash it away.

How can I take a life – even so small,
Who – except for my actions – wouldn't be there at all?

The father is gone. He wants no part
Of this baby I've carried so close to my heart.

My life's just begun. I have nothing to give –
Although I will love her as long as I live.

A couple who wants her – they can't have their own –
Will open their hearts and welcome her home.

The new mom and dad love each other and share
A need for this babe that they'll shower with care.

Grandparents are waiting to hug her real tight,
Protect her from problems she might have to fight.

After searching my soul, there's just one thing to do
That will straighten my life and protect my child too.

I feel GOD used my body – as HE often might do –
To accomplish HIS GOAL and make dreams come true.

In the years that will come, with no guilt I can say:
"I loved her enough to give her away!"

Dedicated to Amanda
Our special "Miracle"
With more love and pride
Than she can even imagine

"GRAMMY"

GOD'S MIRACLE

We had a longing deep inside,
A need we could not fill.
We asked God to help us –
If it could be His will.

He gave to us a baby girl –
So beautiful and fine.
She let us in her tiny heart,
But she took all of mine.

We had a very special bond –
This baby girl and me.
I loved her with my very soul –
This gift from God, you see.

My love for her is in my heart.
A breath away from me.
This love is unconditional
And it will always be.

I pray she will be happy
And feel our constant love,
For she's our special miracle
God sent from heaven above.

THE GIRL WHO INVENTED BABIES

*M*y precious daughter – from the time she could walk and drag a doll around – talked of doing only one thing with her life. She wanted to get married and have "lots of babies." From the time she was seven or eight, she would assemble all the younger children in the neighborhood, sit them on the front steps, and demand their strict attention while "Miss Tammy" taught her class.

Sometime between this era and adulthood, there was a period in which we only knew how her appearance changed by buying her school pictures. She made "Howard Hughes" look like an extrovert. She went to school, came home, and headed to her room to resume her social life via the telephone.

Many times she brought friends home, but usually they were sucked into the deep "Black Hole" of seclusion with her. It was probably for the best since we had reached the stage with which every teenager and mother are well aware – the stage in which if a mother says something is white, the daughter automatically believes it is black. We got along better than most because her friends thought I was "cool."

Due to health problems caused by the medication I took while I was carrying her, she had to have a hysterectomy when she was only twenty years old. She almost had a nervous breakdown at the thought of never having children, and I was so consumed with illogical guilt that I was almost in the same shape she was. She and her husband started immediately to attempt to adopt a child.

After a lot of crying, praying, and searching, GOD rewarded us by giving us the most perfect baby girl we had ever seen. My daughter made the statement that if she had been born with no fingers or toes she would still have wanted her.

As we look back at her early pictures, we realize that like most four-pound babies she looked a lot like a little "alien"; but oh how much she was loved and wanted! It seems that when things look the darkest, GOD steps in to give us what we need.

THE GIRL WHO INVENTED BABIES

There once was a lady
Who wanted a child.
She could not bear one;
She almost went wild.

It was my baby girl
Who each day shed the tears,
So we prayed for a miracle
And GOD calmed our fears.

HE gave a baby girl –
All perfect and new.
This precious babe
Was born 'specially for you –

Not born from your body;
But that is only the start.
Motherhood is a bond
That grows in your heart.

We all needed this baby,
And so we were blessed
'Cause our HEAVENLY FATHER
Sent us HIS BEST.

She's smart and she's pretty;
She's loving and kind.
We thank GOD every day.
She's the best HE could find.

Because she's adopted,
Some people may feel
Our love might be less
Or not be as real.

But in all of our eyes,
She's more special, you see.
She's our MIRACLE gift
GOD planned her to be.

STATIC

*S*ometimes I tend to become complacent and begin to rest upon my "laurels" – as far as my spiritual life is concerned. When this complacency creeps in, my conscious contact with GOD slowly slips away. This gradual process occurs most of the time without me even being aware. People around me usually notice before I do.

Little, insidious things – that is, beginning to skip my morning meditations and forgetting to be grateful for my blessings as well as having more trouble with my personal relationships – are the real "red flags" that finally bring my demand for control painfully back to reality. (There is no such thing as control. Control is an illusion where GOD is involved.) When I try to run my life my way, my priorities get confused.

Before long, I am unable to distinguish between truth and fantasy – illusion and reality. This is when the voices in my head take over. I am confused, irritable, fearful, etc.; and I am no longer any good to others or myself. More importantly, I am no longer useful to GOD.

Only as I pause and ask that GOD'S WILL be done in my life – along with the courage to do IT – does HE calm my fears, quiet the many voices, and allow only HIS VOICE to be audible to me. When this happens, I am given a peace and serenity I had forgotten was possible. The secret is to stay close to GOD. HE is the only true source of POWER.

STATIC

Have you ever traveled late at night,
Riding in your car?
Radio stations making static
Because the stations are too far.

If you keep on driving,
You may see a tower.
The station comes in really clear
Because you're closer to the power.

Some mornings when I wake up,
Things aren't very clear.
I cannot make any sense
Of all the voices that I hear.

As with those stations on the road,
I'm too far from the tower.
On my knees, I talk to GOD
And ask HIM for the POWER.

I ask GOD to bring me close
Since HE only has the POWER.
HIS PLAN for me is always clear
When I am resting by the TOWER.

I WON'T PICK YOUR MATE

I have been proud of the fact that I always have tried to be gracious and cordial to any sweetheart my children brought home. It was usually pretty easy – with a few exceptions – because most of them were wonderful young men and women.

As they got older and their romances took on a more serious posture, they would sometimes "grill me" as to what I thought they should do about a particular candidate. I was wise enough not to venture anything more than a casual, superficial assessment. Sometimes they would be quite irritated with my wanting to be neutral.

From being a teenager myself, I remembered that if my parents disliked someone, it only made me want to protect them and stand by them. Then if they did like someone, it was like the "kiss of death" because I thought they couldn't be very exciting if they didn't ruffle my parents' feathers.

I explained to my children that – even though I usually get very involved in all aspects of their lives – I positively refused to be involved in their selection of a mate for life. I never wanted to be in the position to be blamed for any mistake they might make. This was their responsibility, and they would be the ones required to live with any choice (wise or unwise) they made.

They have made some good choices and some not-so-good choices, but I always knew it was their own choice and I had done my best not to influence them in any way. Thus, the following poem:

I WON'T PICK YOUR MATE

Tell me, please, Mother, what do you think?
I surely like this one; we're right on the brink.

Listen! My child, if you think this one is real,
It's best that you know from the start how I feel.

I promised myself when you started to date
I'll do many things, but I won't pick your mate!!

There are hundreds of chores that a mother should do,
And I've tried my best to do them for you.

I will launder your clothes and tidy your room,
Try lifting your spirits when your heart's full of gloom.

I'll pray for your soul and patch your skinned knee,
But advice on your partner you won't get from me!

If you're really happy, I don't want a voice.
It's none of my business; it's really your choice.

I'll pick out your shirts and your suits and your socks,
But I don't want the blame if your life's on the rocks.

Not everyone felt my choice was the best;
But for forty long years, it's stood the test.

Search your soul, child. Your heart knows what's true.
If you're right for them and they're right for you,

I'll help when I can – whatever your fate.
Just call me "chicken"; I won't pick your mate.

Whoever your mate, this one thing is true:
I'll surely love them because I love you.

Whatever the outcome – either awful or great,
There'll be one thing for sure: You PICKED YOUR OWN MATE!!!

I only ask one thing when I look in your face.
Whoever you choose, that I'll still have a place!

MY 'PRIS'

*M*y older son's wife, Priscilla is very precious to me. People marvel at the relationship we have maintained all of these years – and especially since it grows sweeter and stronger as time goes by.

I remember the first time I saw her. David brought her to a friend's wedding. She had on a beautiful, off-white woolen dress. Her beautiful dark hair and her large dark eyes – so set off by the dress – made her absolutely stunning.

Of course, not being biased at all, I had always known how handsome my son was; but together they were a fantastic-looking couple. I liked her the first time we met, but that admiration has grown into so much more.

Dave and Pris have had the "ups and downs" like all couples (perhaps theirs was a little stormier than most in the beginning), but they love each other very much and have a strong relationship and marriage. The daughter and son they have been blessed with are just as beautiful as you might expect from such a handsome couple.

Wives and mothers-in-laws are commonly like oil and water. They usually feel threatened by each other and are constantly trying to be the most important in the husband or son's life. We have never felt these jealousies. I have my place and she has hers. They are equally important but very different.

We can talk about anything. My son usually has a hard time because we gang up on him. I think we proved how well we get along when we all shared the same house for almost a year. We never had a cross word! We knew when to zig and zag, and we respected each other's privacy.

Pris is more beautiful to me today than the first time I met her; and I thank GOD every day that my son has such a wonderful wife, my grandchildren have such a loving mother, and my husband and I have a "daughter" who loves us. She is always ready to help us any way she can.

I love you "Pris"! Thank you for being the beautiful person you are – inside and out.

MY 'PRIS'

Sometimes when you get "in-laws,"
There is trouble from the start;
But I would like to tell you
About one who stole my heart.

Her beauty is apparent –
Both from the outside and within,
And I am very lucky
To have her for my friend.

I can tell her anything.
We laugh until we're shaking;
But more than that, I know she cares
When I feel my heart is breaking.

I gladly gave my son to her.
She is his loving wife,
The mother of my grandchildren –
So special in my life.

Each day I love her more and more –
Whether I am glad or blue.
Because you're so very special, Pris,
I'm glad WE married you!

DEDICATION

*T*here have been many close friends and relatives over the years who have died. Some of these people were particularly close, and I loved them dearly. I felt a really deep sense of loss at their passing.

One of these special people was my wonderful doctor. He gave me so much care; comfort; support; and yes, even love when I was ill for so long. My life was in jeopardy, and he was at my bedside at all hours of the day and night. He was a great help to me as I struggled with the acceptance of my physical condition.

Dr. Capo was like a father to me. I could go to his office, or he would sit in my hospital room; and we would talk for hours. He often used my room as a place to hide and take a long overdue nap. I still don't know when he slept.

He was a sensitive, caring, and dedicated physician; and he genuinely loved people. He had a fantastic sense of humor, and he was never too busy or tired to care. He understood that sick people are testy and very rarely said anything unkind.

When he died, I felt as if nothing would ever be O.K. again. My heart was broken. This poem is a tribute I wrote for him, and it was published in the hospital newsletter. I was a little fearful that he might take exception to a couple of the lines – even though they were true.

The next time I came to his office for a visit, he came out in the waiting room (which was unusual). He looked at me and said, "In my office NOW!" Fearfully, I followed him into his office; and he shut the door. He said, "Did you write this?" I nodded my head like a frightened child. He grinned and said, "Would you do me the honor of autographing it for me?" I was ecstatic! At his funeral, while his son was reading the poem as part of his eulogy, I thanked GOD that I was allowed to express my feelings for him while he was still alive.

DEDICATION

I have a friend who is as round as he's tall;
But when it comes to doctors, he's the best of them all!

He works very hard, but it seems he just thrives.
I know, with his schedule, he sleeps while he drives.

His work is his life – dedication is all.
He is never too busy to answer a call.

"I have many problems," I'm sure he must say.
"I wonder what new one she'll come up with today?"

But whatever my problems, whatever my plea,
He is never too busy to try and help me.

His interest is real in each patient he treats.
There is a joke and a smile for each one that he meets.

Sick people are testy, and tempers are short;
But he is never impatient. He's just not the sort.

When money is tight, he's the kind of a man
Who says, "Come let me help you! Pay when you can."

When the outlook is bad and danger is grave,
His calming effect makes you want to be brave.

Many times when my heart is aching with fear,
It lightens my burden just knowing he's near.

He takes time for church – not everyone knows;
But his heart's full of love every day 'cause it shows.

There are very few doctors left of his kind.
If you happen to get one, you have made a real find.

You may like your doctor, but mine can't be beat;
And I know that in heaven, he will have a front seat.

GOD'S PLAN

*W*hen my younger son was around thirteen, he and my dad and I went on a trip out west in my dad's Volkswagen camper. We camped many places. The scenery was beautiful and breathtaking. GOD'S SIGNATURE was all around us. My favorite spot was where we camped in Yellowstone National Park.

Even though it was late June when we camped there, the temperature fell to twenty-six degrees at night. From our campfire, we could see the snow-capped tops of the Grand Teton Mountain chain. It was magnificent.

We camped in the park over the weekend. On Sunday evening, they had an open-air church service. The seats were rough-hewn log benches nestled in a thicket of aspen and fir trees, but they did not obstruct the view of the mountains and the river that ran close by.

I got there early; no one was there except me. This may have been the first time I truly was aware of what the Bible means when it says, "BE STILL AND KNOW THAT I AM GOD." GOD revealed HIMSELF to me in a special way as I sat awestruck by HIS handiwork. This poem includes a few of my random thoughts as my mind wandered in this magnificent setting.

GOD'S PLAN

Magnificent trees with a Christmassy smell,
Small, scurrying animals – large ones as well,

A lake full of fish on their way to spawn,
A stately ole doe and her beautiful fawn,

Majestic mountains covered with snow –
When one's in this setting, how could he not know

That GOD'S in HIS HEAVEN, the LORD of it all?
HE makes one tree stand, while another will fall.

The animals know and accept for a fact
Their living and dying as a natural act.

This balance of nature, GOD'S PERFECT PLAN,
Was created around HIS IMAGE called "Man."

If small, little creatures with no wisdom or soul
Can accept GOD'S plan and live life and be bold,

Then with our understanding, why can't we see
GOD gave us this world – with its blessing so free?

So we can be happy if we will be still,
Letting us hear HIS VOICE and knowing HIS WILL.

Unlike the animals, we have a soul.
We have been cast in HIS HEAVENLY MOLD,

Giving HIS SON so our lives will not end,
Living forever if we make HIM our Friend.

KEEPER OF THE FLAME

*R*ecently, I have been going through some very troubling family problems. A member of my family has been the focus of a lot of hurt feelings, and people are not reacting the way they should.

I have struggled through many tears and sleepless nights to try to find a way to make everything right, and it seems there is no answer. I gave the problem to GOD over and over, but I always seemed to take it back. I usually can turn most things over fairly quickly; but as I look back, I can see I was so afraid that I felt God could not handle it and needed my help.

Out of the blue the other day, the picture of Abraham being willing to sacrifice his only son on GOD'S altar came to my mind. I thought about how much faith he showed and how little I had been showing. I have a tendency to forget that GOD loves my family much more than I do and that HE can see the whole picture, while I can see only a minute part. A friend of mine also pointed out that when Abraham bound up Isaac and laid him on the altar, it was an example to us that if we bind our cares together and put them on GOD'S altar, then HE is quite sufficient to bring wonderful things to pass – things we never imagined.

The following poem reminds us that just as fire refines gold or silver, GOD uses fire to refine our hearts. Please, Father, let me always remember that nothing happens in GOD'S WORLD until it is sifted through YOUR HANDS. Thank You, FATHER, for loving us and refining us – even when we kick and scream.

KEEPER OF THE FLAME

Like gold, our spirits are refined
In crucibles of pain.
Sometimes the heat is so intense –
We struggle and complain.

When painful pressure is applied,
We want someone to blame.
Don't we realize our FATHER
Is THE KEEPER OF THE FLAME?

GOD knows our every weakness,
Our desires and things we scheme.
HE always knows just what we need –
Greater things than we could dream.

So take comfort when you're hurting
'Mid your unsuccessful plans.
Nothing ever happens to us
'Til it's sifted through God's hands.

LAST FRUITS ARE ENJOYED MOST

*W*hen my younger son was about thirteen or fourteen, we were doing concessions for an air show in Savannah, Georgia. As he was taking some products out of the refrigerated truck, the door flew back and cut his chin. He had to go to the local hospital for sutures.

After his trip to the hospital, I took him back to the motel where we were staying for him to rest. He lay down on the bed and immediately fell asleep.

He was my last child and was seven and a half years younger than his closest sibling. I always said I had a great system. I loved my older son best because he was my "firstborn"; I loved my daughter the best because she was our only daughter; and I loved the younger son best because he was "our baby."

As I watched him sleep, I felt that warm feeling that is peculiar to motherhood and one with which only another mother can identify. It is the gratitude we feel when we see our child through the eyes of love. It is the special feeling we have when we realize that even with our mistakes, GOD is creating a beautiful human being. I love you Russ.

LAST FRUITS ARE ENJOYED MOST

My baby is sleeping now –
Half man and half boy.
His beauty is flawless;
He's my pride and joy!

He seems so peaceful.
I silently pray
His troubles will never be
More than today.

The world is his oyster;
Every wonder is new.
Each new adventure
Makes his life richer too.

He's loving and caring;
He's witty and smart;
And in only a moment,
He'll capture your heart.

I know life will change things,
And he'll drift away;
But my heart holds the picture
Of him sleeping today.

DON'T MISS IT AGAIN

*N*ow that I am older and none of my children live at home, I sometimes reflect on what kind of mother I was. I was a devoted mother and my children have always meant the world to me. However, I can see many mistakes I made and think of many things that I wish I had done differently. When I am out in the mall or someplace else, I see parents with young children making some of the same mistakes I made; and a wave of sadness washes over me.

There is no harder occupation (or maybe I should say "calling") in the world than being a housewife and a mother. She is on call twenty-four hours a day; and she has chronic fatigue, and her nerves are always frazzled. Usually, as is the case in young families, extra money is not available for outside activities or childcare – unless the mother has full-time employment. Mothers are tied down and feel trapped – no matter how much they love their little ones.

These feelings of frustration cause tempers to be short. There is only time for the things that absolutely have to be done; so everything is rush, rush, and rush! Many moments that should be savored are lost in the shuffle and can never be regained.

When my first granddaughter was born, I made a crewel picture for her nursery. The verse on it was so true: "Go away, cobwebs; dust go to sleep. I'm rocking my baby, for babies don't keep." George Bernard Shaw once said, "It's a shame youth has to be wasted on the young!" It is so true. Our values are honed to a sharper edge as we grow older and our priorities change; but sadly by then, it is usually too late.

I have always believed this is the reason GOD gives us grandchildren. We have a second chance to enjoy and learn the things only children can teach us. We also have a second chance to enjoy and take time for the special joys of a child without the weariness and intense responsibility you feel when you are the parent. I like to tell people: "That is what makes them GRAND children. You can enjoy them, spoil them, and give them back." Thank You, dear LORD, for the second chance.

DON'T MISS IT AGAIN

Do you have a grandchild?
You don't know what you miss –
From their sleepy "good morning"
To that last "good night" kiss.

From the time they awake –
Whether boy or a girl,
They keep your life spinning
In one happy whirl.

They are my heartthrobs –
With their sweet, little voices.
If I could have chosen,
They would still be my choices.

They skip all day long
With so little care.
It's a wonderful world
They allow me to share.

When I'm feeling low,
Their soft, gentle touch
Can make me feel better
And cheer me so much.

GOD sees what we missed
And gives one more chance
To learn from a child
How to make our heart dance.

Bless these precious children.
I pray they never lose
Their zest for life –
Whatever they choose.

Thank You so much
For our fun, happy hours.
They help me remember:
"I must smell the flowers."

PRIORITIES

*O*ne day I was immersed in self-pity – as is usually the case when some facet of my life is not going the way I feel it should. Suddenly, I was yanked up short by a real tragedy in a friend's life.

As I sat and thought about things, I did what I knew I had to do and that was to make a gratitude list. As I made the list, my petty, little problems were so outweighed by my blessings that I became humble and ashamed. I asked GOD to forgive me, knowing full well that self-pity would strike again if I chose to let down my spiritual guard and give Satan even the slightest opening.

We are told we must become as little children if we would be the people our HEAVENLY FATHER would have us to be. My problem is I tend to be CHILDISH rather than CHILDLIKE! Our priorities tend to rearrange in a most dangerous fashion.

PRIORITIES

Sometimes I feel I walk through life
As through a large gift shop.
I stare with great amazement –
When a price tag makes me stop.

A child had helped the owner
To put the tags in place.
He thought he'd done a fine job;
It showed on his little face.

Trinkets with no worth at all
Were priced high and, oh, so wrong;
While works of art were tagged so low –
You could buy them for a song.

It made me want to cry to think
I, so like that little child,

Had marked so very many things
With tags unreal and wild.

We have a set of values;
They develop all our lives.
We force them on our children,
Our husband, or our wife.

Some of the things I value most
May be nothing in GOD'S EYES.
Some things I deem as worthless
May be diamonds in disguise.

How often did a crumpled bill
That we value and call money
Seem to make us take for granted
GOD'S MIRACLE we call "Honey."

Is a shiny car more beautiful
That will wear with every mile –
More beautiful than a toddler's laugh
Or a brand new baby's smile?

Will being heaped with fame and wealth
Mean more to hear and see
Than your child smiling as he says,
"You were always here for me"?

The things we take for granted –
Like GOD'S love and health and friends –
Are the things of greatest value
We'll need 'til our life ends.

So help me, LORD, from this day on,
Place YOUR VALUES in my mind.
Put priorities in their proper place,
So I won't be so blind.

WHERE ARE THE AMERICANS?

*I*t is very seldom I become enraged anymore. After many years of speaking without thinking, I realize it is usually a lesson in futility. It is usually overreaction and better handled with a clear head – after trying to ferret out my part in the conflict. However, yesterday, I chose to make an exception and just plain throw a fit.

My six-year-old granddaughter – who is full of more than her share of creativity, wonder, and enthusiasm that comes with being her age – had received an assignment for her first-grade class. Their teacher had asked them to bring a cap to school to wear all week. They were to pin things on it that were representative of things they enjoyed doing. It seemed like a cute idea, and her mom and I began to try to help her think of appropriate things for her to use. Among the things on her cap was a piano pin (she loves to play on my piano), a teddy bear, and some other things. She added an angel pin which was representative of the fact that she enjoys attending church and Sunday school – as well as the Wednesday night children's group where she learned Bible verses, etc., and receives badges and recognition for her accomplishments.

When she came home the next afternoon, we were all waiting anxiously to hear what reaction she got from her friends about her cap. Sheepishly, she told us she kept her hand over the angel because somewhere (we are still trying to find out where) she had been told she would be sent to the principal's office if anything about church or religion was on her cap. She was afraid. We all tried to explain to her that she should never be ashamed of her faith, but we were not sure we calmed her fears. She was torn by what she was being taught at home and her church and what society, in general, is trying to stifle in her.

I think I might have felt a little like CHRIST felt when HE ran the money-changers out of the Temple. My first reaction was to go and start World War III, but my common sense took over and I decided there must be a better way to get rid of my frustration. That is why I am writing.

It never ceases to amaze me that America's intellectuals will fight to the death to be sure a child has a right to fill their impressionable minds with pornography, sex education, and alternative lifestyles. It is perfectly acceptable to murder

5,000 unborn infants a day because someone was too irresponsible to face the consequences of their lackadaisical and selfish behavior. However, they are frightened to death of biblical truths and do their utmost to keep them away from our children. It seems the BIBLE is the one book that has been banned from our schools and government, and we are all paying the price for it especially the children.

I recently heard of a man when asked, "Why don't you let your child watch network TV?," he simply replied, "The same reason I don't let them drink out of the toilet!" More and more children are turning to lives of crime and degradation. That is all they have been taught by TV (the universal baby sitter), the absence of values taught by GODLY PARENTS, and the glamorization of getting whatever they want in any way they can – except the "old-fashioned way" of working for it.

The things for which we worked for years are now expected the minute a couple is married. At the first sign of a problem or discord, the modern thinking is: "This is hard. We need a divorce." What they have never been taught is that "LIFE IS HARD" and anything worthwhile is worth working for.

As parents and grandparents, we are determined that our children and grandchildren will have things better than we did. Our priorities got all messed up; and in seeing that they had things easier, we have robbed them of the strength it takes to survive in the crazy social arena we have created. We fail to realize we will not always be around to provide their every whim. We have done them a great disservice by instilling in them the belief that life owes them something instead of them needing to give something back. Like a turtle that has lost its shell, they are in constant jeopardy of being ground into an unhappy lump that has no feeling of accomplishment or self-esteem. We were sincere in what we tried to do, but we were sincerely wrong. This has been going on for generations. My parents were not as strong as their ancestors; we weren't as strong as ours; ours aren't as strong as we are. Where will it end? We need to admit to our mistakes and "wake up and smell the coffee." Time is running out!

This country of ours was built on faith in GOD and the unity that comes with all of us working together for the common good. Now they are trying to leave GOD out of our society, and it's every man for himself. I pray that we will see the error of our ways before it is too late.

I want my children and grandchildren to be comfortable as any loving parent would; but if I must choose what is my heart's desire for them, I would and do pray for them every day that they have a right and working relationship with GOD. I want them to realize that only as they put GOD first in their lives can they find real happiness in whatever life circumstances they find themselves.

Peer pressure and popularity are very important to young people today, but they need to realize it is their "standing" with GOD that is most important. Just like the boys in "Pinocchio," who were enjoying all the evils of the world, soon found out, pleasures of this world are very short-lived. Only by standing up and being counted on the side of GOD and the good things they have been taught can they have both a happier life here and, more importantly, in the eternal world to come.

CHILDLIKE

*M*any times God speaks to me in object lessons. Many of these have come in recent years as I observed my grandchildren – with their own agendas, manipulations, tricks, tantrums, and sometimes (less often) their sweet, childlike spirits and unconditional faith. These object lessons range from being hilarious to very touching. Always I see that no matter how our ages vary, our actions are very similar on occasions.

Chronologically, I am a grown woman; but frequently, I can truly identify with the actions of a child. As I watch children relate to their earthly parents, I reflect on how I relate to my Heavenly Father, and there is a definite similarity. Their actions are based on their chronological age; while mine are based on my spiritual age.

The following poem is an example of God's object lesson to me:

CHILDLIKE

I was watching my grandchild –
How she acted at play.
She's only two;
You never know what she'll say.

She poured pieces of puzzle
Out on the floor.
At the very same moment,
"Dad" walked through the door.

Her dad was displeased
At her actions and said,
"Clean up that mess!"
And she tossed her head.

With her hands on her hips –
As she only can do,
She glared at her dad
And said, "I don't have to!"

Well, needless to say,
Her dad took exception
And, with a couple of licks,
Got a different reception.

The child became willing
And wasn't so bold
And decided she might better
Do what she was told.

Then Dad picked her up
And gave her a hug
'Cause his love and her tears
Gave his heartstrings a tug.

Then I saw myself –
As life's pieces I throw,
And God tells me the things
He wants me to know.

With my hands on my hips,
I shout and I whine
and tell Him,
"I don't have to do it this time."

So life gives me some licks
'Cause I insist on my way.
I forget things don't work
If by my rules I play.

So after I'm beaten,
There's a touch from above.
I know I'm forgiven.
I feel God's healing love.

Then I start to wonder
Why I just don't do
The things that MY FATHER
Tells me to do.

But just like that child,
I want to be "boss"
And be in control –
Whatever the cost.

But, thank God, I'm His child –
In spite of my sin;
And He loves and forgives me
Again and again.

THE REAL GIFT

*M*y husband and I have never been overly wealthy in material things such as fancy cars, houses, jewelry, boats, luxurious vacations, etc. – even though we were abundantly blessed with the riches that really matter like family, love, respect, etc. There was never a lot of extra money around – although our needs were always provided.

On our thirty-sixth wedding anniversary, my husband did a catering for 125 people. The couple for whom he catered the party happened to own a jewelry store; so instead of accepting money for the event, he secretly traded out the party for a beautiful strand of matched pearls and a pair of pearl earrings.

He was so proud and happy about the deal, and I was totally touched and thrilled to have such tangible proof of how much he loved me. Since I am a blue jeans or shorts and tee shirt or sweatshirt person, I only wore my pearls on rare occasions and kept them tucked away in the bottom of the antique trunk at the foot of our bed. I felt they were safe.

Recently, we moved into a different house. It was only a coincidence that a couple of months after our move that I went into the trunk to get my blood pressure cuff to take a friend's B/P and I noticed my camera case was empty. With fear and trepidation, I looked for my pearls; and sure enough, everything was gone – only the empty boxes remained. I was heartbroken for myself but even more so for my husband who had sacrificed and worked so hard to give me this token of his love.

As I have learned over the years, resentment over anything only hurts me; so I prayed and asked GOD to help me to be willing to let the hurt and anger go. In HIS TIME, HE answered my prayer. This poem is based on what God helped me to learn from the experience.

THE REAL GIFT

It was our anniversary.
We'd been married many years.
Our love has stood the test of time
Through laughter and through tears.

The wonderful gift he gave me
Was matched pearls of beauty rare.
He was so proud to give this gift –
Proof of his love and care.

They represented sacrifice.
He worked both hard and long
To acquire this most expensive gift,
So to me it could belong.

I kept them in a special place –
I thought safe and secure.
I thought I'd pass them down someday,
So their beauty would endure.

One day I went to look at them –
And to my horror and dismay –
When I opened up the box,
Someone had stolen them away.

At first I felt so very bad.
An emptiness struck my heart.
I thought how badly Rich would feel,
And the tears began to start.

I prayed that GOD would take the pain
And the sense of loss away.
That we both would have what we need –
It became clear that very day.

The real gift my husband gave
Was not the pearls, you see.
They were just a symbol
Of his love and thoughts for me.

Someone could steal away the pearls;
And though it gave me quite a start,
They couldn't take the real gift.
It is locked safely in my heart!

SELF-PITY STINKS

*S*elf-pity is one of the most unattractive and undesirable character defects one can exhibit. Perhaps the reason I feel this way is because this defect is one I exhibit from time to time. The "whining" and the "poor pitiful me" attitude are repulsive to me and any others who must be subjected to it.

I have learned the best way to counteract self-pity (although it is a task I detest and fight as long as possible) is to make a gratitude list. I count my many blessings, starting with the fact that GOD loves me UNCONDITIONALLY and will never abandon me. I am alive; I can see, hear, walk, etc. It never fails to put the voices in my head in accord. We all know how blessed I am.

When I – or anyone else – is immersed in self-pity, we are great tools for the devil. We are accentuating the "negative" and eliminating the "positive." This is the exact opposite of what we are told works to make us happy. No one wants to be around a person with a negative attitude because they tend to bring everyone down before they realize how contagious negativity can be.

I recently heard a story of an Indian brave going to the wise chief and saying, "I feel there is a 'good dog' and a 'bad dog' struggling within me. What should I do?" Without hesitation, the chief answered, "Whichever dog you feed will win." The bad dog is fed with self-pity and the good by gratitude. If we don't make a conscious decision to feed the "good dog," the "bad dog" wins by default.

SELF-PITY STINKS

Dear GOD, I am so angry
When I cannot have my way.
I have so many plans I've made,
But it seems I have no say.

I try so hard to understand
Why things are as they are.
I struggle and I cry a lot,
But I don't get very far.

When I hit my knees to pray,
God will help me do my part –
To be accepting of HIS WILL
With both my head and heart.

So for today I will accept
That GOD is in control.
I don't even need to understand;
I just have to play my role.

"Take away self-pity –
With its garbage and its smell.
Clean me up with gratitude,
So I may serve YOU well."

GREYHOUND! WHAT A DOG!

*M*any events inspire me to verse. One of the main problems I am having getting this book together is that when I have an idea or inspiration, I grab the first thing available to write on, including such things as the backs of envelopes, advertisements, brown paper bags, even toilet tissue. You can see why organizing and making sense of such items is rather difficult.

On this particular occasion, I wrote on the back of an old doctor's receipt in my purse. This poem is in a humorous vein. It never ceases to amaze me the places I get inspired, but my family and friends seemed to enjoy my account of this particular adventure.

I was visiting my son and his family in Indiana, and travel by air was very costly at that particular time. Over the protests of my entire family in three states, I opted to take "Greyhound" since a bus ticket was only about one-third the price of an airline ticket.

It was during the bus strike when snipers were taking "pot shots" at random buses. "Scab employees" were doing the driving within a two-mile radius of the bus depot, and it was interesting to say the least.

Being a firm believer that if your time comes, it can happen as quickly in your sleep as "skydiving," I fearlessly boarded the bus for this ride I will never forget.

GREYHOUND! WHAT A DOG!

I was out of town visiting.
It was time to come home;
So for cheap transportation,
I jumped on the phone.

Airlines were outrageous –
Amtrak even worse.
After fifteen phone calls,
I was ready to curse.

In sheer desperation,
I checked with "Greyhound."
Their prices were good,
So I liked the sound.

In spite of my family
Yelling, "Don't pick it!,"
I proceeded downtown
And bought me a ticket.

On "D DAY" – excited,
I left with a smile.
I hadn't been on a bus
Since I was a child.

An old, cross-eyed blond
And her black gentleman friend –
With two oversized bunnies –
Started settling in.

They intended to take four seats
Instead of just two,
But the bus line insisted
That this wouldn't do.

A couple got on
With a toddler and babe.
What could I say?
I guess they had paid.

The toddler was tied
To his mom with a strap
With continuous screams
From the babe in her lap.

Because of the strike,
A "scab" ground gears and fussed.
His first time apparently,
Driving a bus.

Up the street the real driver,
Who looked like a bear,
Took over the driving —
An answer to prayer.

The raunchy young mother
Fed her babe nature's way.
Attached to her chest
He was happy to stay.

The baby quit crying.
Had she really mothered,
Or was her chest so large
The poor kid just smothered?

The scent of a joint
And booze filled the air.
The B.O. and boom boxes
Also were there.

'Bout five miles out of town –
On our way at long last,
The bus screams to a halt.
We had to buy GAS!

The back row of seats
And half up the aisle,
The natives were restless
And began to get wild.

The big, burly driver
Stopped and went to the back.
Firmly, he warned them
This was no way to act.

We were moving again.
I couldn't be prouder,
But the noise from the back
Only got louder.

The bus turned around.
It was so irritating.
Back at the station,
Four police cars were waiting.

Ten cops came on board.
Don't ask me how.
Five guys won a free night
At the local "hoosegow."

We started again.
In less time than it took
To read through a chapter
Of a very small book,

The brakes started squealing.
I don't mean to be rude;
But the obese, ole driver
Had to have food.

My seatmate got off.
There was no one to grab it.
As you probably guessed,
I got stuck with a rabbit!

I fell asleep.
Guess the booze was still flowing
'Cause when I awoke
A fistfight was going.

Then once again,
The brakes started squeaking;
And off to a phone,
'Ole Smokey was streaking.

Three more blue lights
Through the night did appear,
And we lost six more "rowdies"
Out of the rear.

After layovers, more stops,
And things to deter,
The driver announced
How brave that we were

To be riding the bus
'Cause strikers might snipe;
But what went on inside
Was my biggest gripe.

Three hours late,
We finally arrived,
Saying our "thank yous"
'Cause we were alive.

My mortified son
Was on time to meet me
But threatened, if anyone saw us,
He'd beat me.

Though the rabbit and I
Were about the same size,
He was the same,
But I was more wise.

'Cause next time I must travel,
I won't make a fuss
When my sweet family says,
"Leave the driving to us!!"

CAN I ASK YOU SOMETHING?

When one of my granddaughters was around five years of age, she discovered what older girls have always known: how much fun it is to talk on the telephone. For the first few months, my number and the number of our business (where her dad and grandfather worked) were the only numbers she had committed to memory; so she called us a lot.

My phone was constantly ringing. It rang every time I was out on the deck, when I was on the other line, when I was in the shower, etc. Even though it was sometimes inconvenient, it was always a pleasure to hear her sweet, little voice saying, "Grammy, can I ask you something?" This same question would come up many times in our conversations. Sometimes it was difficult not to get exasperated – no matter how I fought against it.

On one occasion when I was wrestling with a personal problem, I had so many questions. I wanted to question GOD; but because of my age and experience, I knew the answers would come in HIS TIME. I realized, however, there was not a lot of difference in my granddaughter and me. I immediately prayed and asked GOD to help me be as patient and kind to her as He is to me.

I love you Casey! I thank GOD every day that you are so healthy and intelligent and have such a beautiful and inquisitive mind.

CAN I ASK YOU SOMETHING?

Many times on the phone,
I hear my granddaughter say,
"Can I ask you something?" –
As she stops in her play.

Then she asks me a question
That seems silly to me;
But it's something to her
That seems big, don't you see!

So I stop what I'm doing
And listen to hear.
Is her question for knowledge
Or prompted by fear?

The questions keep coming,
And patience wears thin.
You think she's all finished,
And she asks you again.

"Can I ask you something?"
I know this is the way
That she learns and she grows
Day after day.

As I lay in the dark
And ponder my day,
I suddenly realize
That I'm the same way.

Time after time
As I wonder and fear,
I snuggle up close
And hope GOD will hear:

"Can I ask You something?"
Do YOU really love ME?
Do YOU care what I do –
If I am happy and free?

"Can I ask You something?"
Will YOU always be near
When I am afraid and
Smothered with fear?

"Can I ask YOU something?"
Will YOU give what I need
If I ask for YOUR GUIDANCE
And YOUR RULES I heed?

"Can I ask YOU something?"
When I mess up and sin,
Will YOU forgive me
And help me again?

How can a child's questions
Burdensome be
When I realize
She's so much like me?

"Can I ask YOU something?"
Will YOU help me be kind
And answer her questions
Like YOU answer mine?

OLD DOGS AND NEW TRICKS

*W*ell, here I am being catapulted into the twenty-first century. You may be sure I am doing so, kicking and screaming all the way. Some of my friends, who know me rather well, say I have a tendency to put off the inevitable changes that life throws my way. Personally, I prefer to think that every time I learn something new and begin to feel comfortable with it, someone comes up with a "better idea." Each time I have to put my old brain into overdrive and wrestle with something new. Keeping a point on a #2 pencil is still a little tough for me.

Admittedly, with each new innovation, I never seemed to learn to perform it until I was completely abandoned by my teacher. Examples consist of everything from starting an I.V. infusion to making cotton candy.

My reluctance to change is well known to my family. I guess the events of last Christmas should not have been the surprise, trauma, and frightening experience they were. My younger son, who has no fear, set out to assure himself that I would not sneak back to my word processor when he went back to his home in South Florida. He took my beloved word processor (with a monitor) that I was just feeling at ease with, boxed it up, secured it shut with almost a whole roll of duct tape, and banished it to the basement. He put it in an obscure spot that I have yet to find. He left me with these words: "Learn the computer, or use a pencil!" I have always suspected he is a "bad seed" and should have been eaten at birth like a young "guppy."

With my word processor, you pushed a button, and it came on; you pushed the same button, and it went off. (So what's wrong with simple?) With this new-fangled contraption, IT tells you when you can turn it on and IT tells you when IT is ready to be turned off. I am learning there are dire consequences if you choose to defy its commands. There is something very intimidating about being ordered around by a machine.

Well, they tell me this is progress. However, it has taken me two hours to do what I could have done on my trusty word processor in fifteen minutes. However, with all of the helpful hints I am receiving from the damnable machine – that is, RUNNING WITH SCISSORS MAY BE DANGEROUS – it will be a snap to teach this "OLD DOG" new tricks.

By the way, what was Y2K????

MAKE ME A CHILD AGAIN

*O*n January 11, 1990, we had a wonderful blessing come into our lives. We already had been blessed with two beautiful granddaughters; so it was really special when our grandson, Zachary David Poe, made his appearance in the world.

Like his sister, he was born by C-section and announced his arrival with a loud and lusty cry as soon as his head popped free. For the second time, it was my privilege to be the first in our family to hold him. As before, I took him over to his mom and dad. We were all ecstatic to have a little boy to carry on the family name.

He has always been a sweet and loving child who liked to be hugged and cuddled. He walked around the house with a bottle of milk hanging out of his mouth until he was almost two years old. Suddenly, he threw the bottle away and, to our knowledge, has not been known to drink milk since that time.

Zach has always been mechanically inclined, loving anything that had wheels and moved noisily. He is all boy!

He is extremely intelligent; but at the age of three, he still only jabbered in what we called "Zachinese." We decided he might have a real problem, so he was taken to a speech therapist who validated our fears that he indeed did have a problem. Through a friend of mine, I learned the county school system had a program for his particular problem and they have a very high success rate.

So at age three, he started to public school. He rode the special education bus; and the first time I saw him climb on that yellow bus, I thought I would die. He had marvelous teachers; and it seemed to us they "flipped a switch," and he began to talk. Sometimes now we wonder where the switch is to "cut him off." We are amused sometimes when he is talking and his English is so correct. We laugh and say, "Nobody will ever think he learned to talk from us." He's never "mad"; he is "angry," etc.

He is very friendly and introduces himself to everyone around. He sticks out his hand and says, "I'm Zachary Poe. Who are you?" Before long, he has worked the whole room and knows most everyone there.

Zach is very much like his grandfather, or "Pop," as everyone calls him. He, too, works a room with seemingly great ease and effortlessness.

He is very close to Jesus, and he takes asking GOD for help seriously. One day I had lost my car keys, and I was getting most perturbed. Zach said, "Grammy, have you asked Jesus to help you find them?" I did, and they were found in a matter of seconds. It is embarrassing when a ten-year-old has to point out something that you should be doing every day.

There is a general consensus in our family that he will be either a politician or a preacher. He has a sweet, loving spirit; and we hope it will be the latter, but a politician with these qualities would render a valuable service. At the risk of sounding harsh, it might be a refreshing change.

He is a beautiful child with huge brown eyes and coal black hair. In the movie "Pinocchio" when the wooden puppet turned into a real boy, the real boy looked exactly like our Zach. Pinocchio was touched by fairy dust; and we know our precious, little boy was touched by "angel dust" to make him so special.

Most of the time when we are having meals together, he is the one who is usually elected to say "Grace." Even though he is thirteen years old now, I can still see him with his big brown eyes and his jet black hair as he looked as a child of four or five when he said this blessing. Times are tough for children in this day and time; and our prayer for him is that he will keep his sweet, loving spirit and use it to honor his HEAVENLY FATHER.

MAKE ME A CHILD AGAIN

"GOD is great and GOD is good,"
My little grandson said –
Just the same as years ago
His dad, my son, had said.

"Let us thank HIM for our food" –
Tiny hands folded in respect.
I saw his precious head bowed low,
And I started to reflect.

DEAR LORD, if we could only be
Again like this sweet child
Whose heart is still so tender,
So fresh from YOUR DEAR SMILE.

They know no hate; they know no fear.
Their joy and love run free.
Their honesty and faith abound.
Please give these traits to me.

They don't know how to worry.
They feel no need to lie.
They jump and play; and at night, they pray,
"Take my soul if I should die."

When times are hard and we're afraid,
We ask, "Why this abuse?"
Childlike faith will help us pray,
"Help this heartache serve some use."

Sometimes in our self-pity,
We can't see GOD'S smiling face.
If we stop and look around,
It's everywhere and every place.

It happens in such subtle ways.
We often miss HIS CUE
When HE says to us, "Let this one help.
I put them there for you."

So tenderize my heart, DEAR LORD,
And help me "childlike" be
And see again that "GOD IS GOOD"
And always cares for me.

SPIRIT OF ELECTIONS PAST

esterday was Election Day; and it is all over but the shouting, the backbiting, and the new and inventive ways for each party to bash their opponents. They must form new gridlock to keep our country from going forward or, worse yet, totally grinding to a halt. The important thing nowadays seems to be to see which side can dig the deepest in the mud to tear down the winners (of either party) and how to build up and soothe the shattered egos of the losers. It would be wonderful if we could just all be AMERICANS that love our country and want to work together to make this nation strong, loved, and respected as it once was.

Happily, I grew up in an era in which television was not a factor. My father and uncle were both very political and had quite a bit of "clout" in our county and surrounding counties. I can remember them going from house to house to ask people to vote for their candidates. Their agenda, however, did not include mudslinging and deliberate lies to make their respective points. They simply stated their case and gave their friends and neighbors the respect and opportunity to make their own decisions.

My dad, who was ninety-four on April 7 and still has a mind like a steel trap, spent yesterday serving as a deputy in a polling place in his county. He works at the polls every time there is an election, and he loves it. He enjoys talking with all of his friends that he might not have seen since the last election. The office of voter registration gave him a plaque for his many years of service, and he was very proud. Being a "Yellar Dog" Democrat, I know it is hard for him not to nudge voters toward the Democratic booths. Even more than a Democrat, he is an honest, patriotic citizen. He holds democracy and one's right to choose his own candidates in higher esteem than anything except his spiritual beliefs.

I became very nostalgic last evening as I flipped from channel to channel on the television. Every station was inundated with returns, predictions, criticisms, and hype. Today those same channels pushed PROZAC stock up fifty points by telling us all of the depressing things that are in our future because of this candidate or that candidate, depending upon the party to whom you are listening.

I kept thinking about Anne Murray's song that says, "Wouldn't it be nice to have a little GOOD NEWS today?" We are not even allowed one day to reflect on the fact we are blessed enough to live in a free country in which voting is a privilege before we are slapped in the face with the fact that so many people are so disgusted with politics in general that they choose apathetically not to even exercise this wonderful privilege so many have died to protect. Twenty years or so ago, I stood in line for five hours to vote in a presidential election. My next-door neighbor, who had escaped from behind the IRON CURTAIN on his second attempt (he was shot and wounded and recaptured on his first attempt) and had to wait several years for his second attempt, was in line right behind me. Some of those in line got tired and began to leave. I'll never forget what he said, "When you come from a place like the one I escaped from, you will realize what a gift democracy is and nothing could keep you from voting."

I hate all of the lies and name calling that come with an election. Yet as one great patriot put it: "I MAY NOT AGREE WITH WHAT YOU SAY, BUT I WILL DEFEND TO THE DEATH YOUR RIGHT TO SAY IT!"

When I was in elementary school and high school, we had newspapers, radios, and political rallies (or SPEAKINGS as we used to call them) to keep us informed. Election time was a source of great fun and camaraderie. On Friday and Saturday, we would all pile in the car and go to a "speaking." It was a great social occasion. The grownups would take chairs and listen to the candidates. Usually, the platform for the speakers was the back of a flatbed truck that doubled as a bandstand for a guitar and banjo picker who played "Happy Days Are Here Again" on cue. Being in northwest Florida, where seafood was plentiful, there was usually an "all you can eat" fish fry to help draw a crowd. All of us kids would run around playing games and eating junk we all brought. Finally, it would get so late that we would pile in our respective cars and go to sleep. Strangely, the next morning we would awaken in our own beds.

I came from a small town and county where everyone knew everyone else. Therefore, you had to keep your political views to yourself because you never knew what cousin, sister, or brother-in-law, etc., of the candidate might over-hear our pubescent opinions. Everyone knew these opinions came straight from our parents.

Election night rated right below Christmas and Halloween as a social occasion. About 7 p.m., we would all walk down to the county courthouse and wait for the returns. There were no electronic calculators back then, and each vote was counted by hand. Sometimes it would be 3 or 4 a.m. before the outer edges of the county got their votes counted and in – to be added to the others. There was a huge chalkboard on which the names of all the candidates were listed, and they updated it as each new ballot box was received and counted. I picture it as something like the New York Stock Exchange – and for the popula-tion of our county, just as important!

The father of one of my dearest childhood friends was sheriff of our county for years, so his race was very important to us. We stayed to the bitter end to see if he had been re-elected. One time his opponent was the man who ran the local pool hall. He received a ridiculously small number of votes. The day after the election, he walked around with a gun and holster around his waist. He said, "If I don't have more friends than that, I NEED PROTECTION."

The fact that we would roller skate around the courthouse sidewalks and take turns sliding on cardboard boxes on the steep, grassy hills the landscape afforded would help to entertain us and alleviate any moments of drowsiness that might try to overtake us on this special evening. Only the faint of heart would admit they were sleepy – even though it was hours past our bedtime.

Our house was only two blocks from the courthouse, so sometimes my mom and dad would take us home to bed. When we were asleep, my dad would sneak out, go back, and wait for the final results to share in the rejoicing – or the weeping and wailing as the case might be.

I remember vividly the year Eisenhower defeated his Democratic opponent. It had been ingrained in us that a REPUBLICAN president would be a greater catastrophe than a world war. I was actually relieved when the newspapers came the next day and did not mention "bread lines" forming that afternoon. As I grew older, I realized this line of thinking came from the GREAT DEPRESSION that my parents and their peers had endured. Because there was a REPUBLICAN president in office when the Depression began and then a DEMOCRAT (Franklin D. Roosevelt) was elected and things got better, it was a natural feeling for them to have.

I remember the day when FDR died. My family, as well as millions of other families, cried as if they had lost a close family member. Of course, I am not Catholic; but no POPE was ever mourned like their great leader, savior, and friend.

Well, back to the present. For weeks, I had been listening to all of the negative campaigning. If only one-tenth of what they say about each is true, it seems impossible to elect anyone who stands for the principles upon which our country was founded. All of the information I received was pretty depressing, and it would have been easy to become "apathetic" – like so many others – and say, "What's the use? My vote is not going to make any difference at all." Then I remembered Madelyn Murray O'Hare only needed 10,000 people to take prayer out of the schools. I am still wondering where we all were when that happened. It seems evil is more motivated than it used to be, and it lulls us into this apathy that will take away all of the wonderful liberties we take for granted.

We must not let them win. We can already see in what chaos our country now operates. Evil wins when we follow the "line of least resistance."

As I went into the voting booth that day, I said a prayer, put the little stylus in the holes, and asked GOD for HIS WILL to be done. If I were not spiritual enough to truly believe GOD is in charge and it really does not matter what we do as long as we try to do the next right thing as we feel it to be (the results are up to HIM), I probably would have given up long ago. My son took my granddaughter in the booth with him because he wanted her to have the experience of what an election is about. He let her punch a whole page on the ballot because they were all incumbents and had no opponents. She was nine at the time, and she got her "I VOTED" sticker and was very proud. I told my son I felt I had voted the same way she did – without a clue.

Behaving as an adult is sometimes hard for me. Once in awhile, my childish side takes charge and I do some pretty strange things. When I chose what I would wear to vote, I chose my sweatshirt with the clown on the front.

As I signed my ballot, I pushed the little music box in the sleeve that plays "Send in the Clowns"! Not everyone understood the significance, but a few folks standing near me began to smile because they caught my drift.

Just let me say: With all of its flaws, democracy is the greatest gift we have as Americans. I thank GOD I have the opportunity to live "in the land of the free and the home of the brave." It is my firm belief that it is our duty to pray for our elected officials – no matter what party they come from – and ask GOD'S GUIDANCE for them.

GOD BLESS AMERICA! You may be interested to know that I wore my "I voted" sticker just as proudly as my granddaughter did because I felt I had done my patriotic duty, and that always feels good.

CALL COLLECT

*B*eing a recovering "TELEPHONE ADDICT," one of the most important comforts of my life is to know that – no matter where I am, whether I have good news or bad news to share – I have people I can depend on. Even though I spend much of my life walking an emotional and, most of the time, a physical tightrope – if I get in a jam, they will be there.

One of the ways I know these people will be there is – no matter where I am, whether I have a penny to my name, whether I am being a pest or I am in real trouble – is that if I need to call them collect, I will always hear them say, "Sure, I'll accept the charges!" The person I feel the most comfortable doing this with is my father in Florida. He is always glad to hear from me. The sound of my voice is all the repayment he will ever want. He is always there, waiting to help me any way he can – without any thoughts of anything except his child needs something and he can't wait to oblige. Being sixty-five years old, I try not to impose on his generosity unless it is necessary; but it is great to know I have that "safety net" of love, support, and availability.

My dad is a very young 94 year old who puts most young men to shame. I know he can't live forever, but I will always be grateful for the example he has given me so that when something does happen to him I will not have lost my "safety net"!

He taught me by example that I have a "HEAVENLY FATHER" who is always available and is so anxious to hear from me. He has resources and answers to all of our problems, and He wants to know WE know we need HIM. The beautiful part is that HE is ALWAYS available and the call is always free.

CALL COLLECT

When you were young,
Was there ever a day
When pitfalls and obstacles
Lined life's highway?

You tried your resources,
And they never worked.

If you called on your friends,
They seemed busy and irked.

When you'd done your best
And given up in despair,
There was Father at home
Who always would care.

So you'd swallow your pride
'Cause you knew you'd been wrong,
And you'd dial that old number
You'd neglected so long.

With your heart in your throat –
Each hair standing erect,
"Sure! I'll take it," Dad answers,
"Yes, I know it's collect."

"Don't worry," Dad tells me.
And I know right away
That whatever my troubles
They'd all be O.K.

Our HEAVENLY FATHER sits on HIS throne
And patiently waits by his HEAVENLY PHONE
To hear from His children who struggle and fret –
Too proud to request all the help they could get.

By dialing HIS NUMBER
And telling Him all our fears,
He'll rebuild our lives
And dry all our tears.

He wants us to call.
HIS SON paid the bill,
And our lives will be better
When we do HIS WILL.

So stay close to God;
And when you need assistance,
It won't cost as much
'Cause it won't be long distance!!!

ANYTHING BUT PAY THE CHECK

*M*y dad has had the habit for many years of meeting with all of his old cronies at one of the local restaurants. They drink coffee and sit and discuss everything from the going interest rate, oil speculation in the county, sports, and even politics when they are really feeling brave.

Usually the other guys – to see what kind of rise they can get out of my dad – gang up on him. This especially happens when they start talking politics since, as everyone who knows him is aware, my dad is a "Yellar Dog Democrat" and nothing will ever change that. When I was growing up, it was ingrained in me that "if a jackass is running on the Democratic ticket, you better vote for them." Many have and he did; but of course, to be honest, jackasses are not limited to the Democratic Party.

One particular morning as they drank coffee at a restaurant called "Baker's Steak House," my dad passed out on the floor and had to be given CPR. His pulse dropped down to thirty, and an ambulance was called. He was whisked away for the immediate insertion of a cardiac pacemaker.

Needless to say, all of his friends were very alarmed and very relieved when they found out he was going to be fine. After we were sure he was going to be fine, I wrote this little poem to cheer him up. Of course, his friends loved it.

ANYTHING BUT PAY THE CHECK

Baker's Steak House was buzzing
That morning with chatter.
The BOARD OF DIRECTORS
Was discussing a matter.

We know men don't gossip.
If you think so, you're wrong.

It's real information
They meet to pass on.

After cups were refilled
Many times on that day,
They began to discuss the check
And who'd pay.

Ole Rube didn't offer.
He had nothing to say
'Cause strangely he felt himself
Slipping away.

He slumped to the table
And then to the floor.
An ambulance was called.
He was whisked out the door.

His friends were concerned.
They feared he was dead,
But a pacemaker saved him
Marked "FULL SPEED AHEAD!"

He's doing fine now –
Even better than new.
However, the moral
To this story is true.

Every person on earth –
Whether wise man or jerk –
Has his own personality
With its own little quirk.

We all love Ole Rube;
But with no disrespect,

He'll do anything
Before PAYING THE CHECK!!!

THIS PROBLEM

I have mentioned before that my life changed dramatically when I became "physically challenged." (I hate the terms "handicapped" and "disabled.") I am not disabled because I feel that mentally and spiritually I am much more sensitive and capable since my health has deteriorated.

It was a long time before I quit asking "WHY" and began to really believe God had a better plan for me and my life. The problem is not the issue but how I accept and handle it that determines whether it is a liability or an asset.

In my opinion, each of God's children are challenged in one way or another. No one knows the way that someone else is being challenged, and that is just one more reason we should be nonjudgmental and kind to those around us. I like the adage that says, "Never judge an Indian until you have walked three days in his moccasins."

THIS PROBLEM

Dear God, I have this problem
That seems so large to me.
It has rearranged my whole life.
From its grip, I can't get free.

My pride and independence
Have always had control.
This problem that enslaves me
Has reversed my every role.

My role has been "caretaker"
To meet the others' needs.
I had all the answers –
If my advice they'ed heed.

Now God has a different role,
A new part I need to learn

If I'm to be His vessel –
My "butterfly wings" to earn.

My problem is a long-term one.
It's most likely here to stay.
Only I can make the choice
How to handle it each day.

If I avoid self-pity
And get out of my way,
God comes in and all goes well.
It's MY choice how long HE'LL stay.

Father, help me to be willing
To accept and not ask "WHY?"
Then I'll be happy every day.
That's God's promise if I try.

TWO KINDS OF PRIDE

*P*ride is listed at the top of the list of the seven deadly sins in the Bible. Pride is synonymous with ego. Pride causes many negative actions and reactions that bring pain to others as well as myself. Pride makes it impossible for me to say things that I have to say to be happy and serene in my life. Two examples are: "I don't know" and "I'm sorry"! Pride prompts an illusion of inflated intelligence that tricks me into believing I am an authority on every subject.

There is another kind of pride, however, that is good. It tells me I am a worthwhile human being – endowed with potential, talents, and usefulness to God. It is self-esteem that helps me develop whatever assets God has given me. In that way, I can be the person God intended and know the joyous satisfaction that comes only with flexing and fulfilling my potential with God's help.

Ego has been known as EASING GOD OUT and attempting to take control of our lives. SELF-ESTEEM is realizing that everything we have is a gift from God and causes us to humbly offer our talents and every facet of our lives to God for His use as HE sees fit. The following poem is about these two kinds of pride:

TWO KINDS OF PRIDE

Some days are quite simple –
As serene as can be.
All's right in God's world,
And I'm happy and free.

As I ponder the question
As to why this might be,
It never fails;
The answer's in me.

There are two kinds of pride –
One good and one bad.
The one in control
Makes me happy or sad.

There's a good kind of pride
That's healthy for man.
It's our self-esteem,
And it's part of God's plan.

This kind of pride
Makes us stand up and see
The joyous examples
God wants us to be.

But the other pride tells us:
"Do it your way! Have fun!
You're the real 'boss.'
You don't need anyone!"

Just as soon as I fall
For this ole "ego trip,"
My life falls apart,
And I start to slip.

As I'm flat on my back –
Feeling I'm such a jerk
'Cause I've tried something again
That never does work,

I pray to remember
What pride's meant to be:
"A gift that YOU give us,
Not what I take for me!"

LETTING GO

*T*he hardest part of being a parent is learning to let go. If we did our parenting job well, letting go and letting our child make his own mistakes and decisions would be the climax or the pinnacle of our job.

With each passing year of our child's life, we are practicing in various small and then larger ways to help our child become self-sufficient and a productive member of society.

It is only normal that at such an important and special time we naturally should have some fear. We question how they will handle life without us. We wonder if our training and the values we tried to instill will be sufficient as they step over the threshold of adulthood.

This is an emotional time for both the parent and the child. If we can "let go" gracefully, if we have shown them love and respect and they honestly feel we believe they are capable of achieving anything they are willing to work for hard enough, we all will reach a new and satisfying plateau in our lives. We will always be important in our children's lives – but not in such a prominent way as when they were younger.

Only as we learn to "let go" can we "hold on." We, as good parents, must always be available for support – but not as a crutch. "Letting go" is a difficult process because we all are learning the rules and learning to set boundaries. However, if we all treat each other with understanding and respect, it can be a beautiful time of transition.

LETTING GO

When a baby arrives – all fragile and small,
You worry for fear you might hurt him.
He cries and you cringe; you pray and you pace.
You're tempted to just plain desert him.

With each little coo and smile you receive,
The strings on your heart are pulled tighter.

When he takes his first steps, you're bursting with pride.
Your hopes for him couldn't be brighter.

When school starts, you send him out all alone.
You're sure that your heart is breaking.
Although he seems small, he feels so big.
You're proud of the progress he's making.

With each passing year, his accomplishments grow;
But his needs still center 'round you.
Then all of a sudden – it seems so soon,
He's grown! With a new point of view.

These strings so entwined must suddenly break,
And it hurts when you finally know
The hardest part of a mother's role
Is when she has to let go.

If you try to hang on 'cause you see their mistakes,
You drive them further away;
But grit your teeth and dry your tears
And remember that you had your day.

The strings that are broken are the strings that were choking
Independence you claimed that you tried for;
But it's hard to give up that special control
Or their constant needs that you strived for.

Only letting go makes the special strings
Of love and respect grow tighter.
If you loosen your hold, you can bank it like gold
That their flame of love will grow brighter!!

All children, for years, have been quite convinced
That their growing up has been such a strain;
While each mother knows that only her heart
Has suffered and felt so much pain.

But when it's all over and the pain is all done,
There's one thing you know is quite true.
Their love and their caring, they'll always be sharing
Because you're not one life – you're two!!

GOOD OLE DAYS

A few years back, a high school friend of mine laughingly told me about the great change that had taken place in his mother's habits since he married and left home. His mother had always been a real home-maker and made everything from "scratch." She spent many tiresome hours in meal preparation.

Since my friend had left home, his father had retired. They had bought a motor home and had begun to travel around the country with a camping group. They were having a wonderful time; and because of all the travel, she began to learn many shortcuts to make her life simpler.

Months after she began taking these shortcuts and they had become a matter of course, her son, my friend, came home for a visit and he was amazed. I knew and loved his mother for many years, so I found his story most amusing. Her new course of action inspired this poem. She had a good laugh, too, and took it and shared it with many of her camping friends.

GOOD OLE DAYS

Remember the ole days when we were just kids
And it took so much time to do things that we did?

The older folks told us in so many ways
How much rougher they had it back in their days.

Everything is so handy – we can't even guess
The differences now with which we are blessed.

Vacation rolled 'round, and I went home and saw
'Bout these things that I heard from my kids' grandma.

We got there for breakfast; and to my surprise,
"Ole Instant Grandma" sure opened my eyes.

The first course was juice – not much of a chore.
It was straight from the can; she doesn't squeeze anymore!

There were piping hot biscuits out of the pan –
Not big like her old ones; tiny ones from a can!

No homemade butter is served on your bread.
We can't afford butter! Are you out of your head?

The bacon was quick; oh, the time that she saved
By popping it all in her new microwave.

Eggs can be harmful, so we must stay away.
Phony imitations are the price we must pay!

Grits that I love used to be such a chore.
Now they're so simple with boiling water to pour.

The coffee is silent; you don't hear it perk.
To waste all that time you'd be such a jerk!

There's imitation cream and, for sure, Sweet and Low.
We do what we can to cut calories, you know.

With disposable napkins for wiping my chin,
I secretly smiled – my meal to begin.

Amazed but still hungry, I just couldn't wait –
'Til "Ole Instant Grandma" served my paper plate!

After we'd eaten – the trash thrown away,
I began to reflect on what I'd learned today.

The "Ole Instant Grandma" has amended her ways.
She's sure learned a lot since the quote "good ole days."

So if things can be easier, go on and rig it
'Cause "Ole Instant Grandma" surely can dig it!!!

HE'S YOURS NOW, LORD

*F*rom the moment your child arrives, you begin to think about and dread the time when he will leave the nest. This time is especially traumatic when it is your last child.

People have said when death is imminent, your whole life flashes before your eyes. Having never been quite that close to death, I do not know if this is or is not true. However, I can testify to the fact that when your last child's car backs out of the driveway to attend college that **his** life definitely flashes before a mom's eyes.

There are some very ambivalent feelings that happen at this time. You are filled with pride that your child has progressed enough to enter a new and exciting stage of his development. You are thankful he is ready to leave home to tackle new challenges and adventures. Nevertheless, you experience a great deal of fear and sadness that he is leaving the care and protection of his family. You feel helpless; you pray that all of the values you tried to instill in him will hold up against the freedom and peer pressure he must now face on a daily basis.

To have any serenity at all, you must truly "let go and let GOD." You pray GOD will give him what he needs, and you take comfort in the fact that he was always GOD'S child. He was only on loan to us. You know you want nothing but the best for him. You also know GOD loves him far more as "HIS HEAVENLY FATHER" than you do as his "finite earthly parent." This truth is the only thing that can set you free from your anxiety and fear. If you can free yourself of your insecurity, then you can be grateful that GOD put this beautiful creature in your life and loaned him to you for awhile.

HE'S YOURS NOW, LORD

My last little boy went to college today.
Logic says he should go, but I want him to stay.

He was excited but did not want it to show.
I kept back the tears: "It's so hard to let go."

He's strong and he's healthy and really quite smart –
And being my baby, he's the key to my heart.

As he sat in the car, all I could see
Was his first day in school when he had to leave me.

I can still see his short pants and little fat knees
As he sat on the couch, looking out at the trees.

He tried not to cry, but he was so scared –
That was a feeling that he and I shared.

I knew he'd be fine, but I felt so bad
'Cause he was the last little baby I had.

When he drove away, I said, "I love you, Russ."
He gave me a wave that said, "Mom, don't make a fuss."

I've done my best, LORD, with all my mistakes.
I know, with YOUR HELP, he'll have what it takes.

So I'll give him to You, LORD, because he is a man
And I've taken care of him as long as I can.

Please, God, keep him safe and let Your will be
'Cause I know that YOU love him much more than me.

STONE MOUNTAIN AND ME

*W*hen I was about twelve or thirteen years of age, my parents, my younger brother, and I visited Atlanta on a family vacation from Florida. At this time, there was no Stone Mountain Park – with all of the beauty and attractions that are now there. There was a partial carving on which some stonecutters were working. There was a sandy area at the foot of the carving where a handful of "gawkers" would stop and watch them at work.

Years later, after I had my own family, my husband was transferred to Atlanta. One Sunday afternoon, we revisited the park and I was totally amazed by what had been created. We all admired the park, the carving, etc. but didn't give it much thought after we left there.

Sometime later we were in the concession business, a sideline for both my husband and me. He was a comptroller with Sears, and I was a Registered Nurse. We enjoyed being out on weekends in the fresh air while meeting and interacting with many new people.

Many times early in the morning and many times late at night, I would be driving by the carving with the lights shining on it and each time it seemed more beautiful. One day I was driving into the park just as the sun was rising, and I had a spiritual experience. I had been obsessing, fretting, and worrying about some painful changes that were taking place in my life when suddenly I looked up and saw the carving. GOD put a wonderful message in my heart, and I immediately knew that everything was going to be okay. HE reminded me that only through pain do we seek GOD'S COMFORT and that the freedom and peace that come from this painful refining in our lives produces the only true beauty we are able to obtain. I remember that message every time I see the mountain on a visit or even in a photograph.

STONE MOUNTAIN AND ME

There once was a large granite rock in the ground.
Few folks even noticed that it was around.
Once in awhile, somebody would say,
"That's a big rock." Then they went on their way.

The big rock was happy with its lowly existence.
The last thing it wanted was outside assistance!
But one day men came – stonecutters by trade,
And into that rock they started to wade.

With chisels and tools, they'd hammer each day;
While the big rock just hoped that they'd go away.
They would stop for awhile; the big rock would smile;
But they always came back. Seems that was their style.

The hammer and chisels were painful, you see.
The big rock said, "Why should this happen to me?"
But one day the rock saw a pattern take form.
It liked what it saw, and its feelings were warm.

The work was all finished; the old rock had been changed.
A great work of art had now been arranged.
The once scattered few – with their casual glance –
Were joined by great throngs when they had a chance.

What seemed so painful and unfair at the start
Made this rock a great mountain – all set apart.
Just like with the mountain, GOD gets out HIS TOOLS
And chisels our lives by HIS BOOK OF RULES.

The things that seem painful and cruel just may be
What will bring out the beauty in you or in me.
If we trust HIM completely when the going gets tough,
We become beautiful – HIS GEMS IN THE ROUGH!

MY RICH, THE OPTIMIST

I am a Registered Nurse; and my husband, before his retirement, was a controller for a large national company. Because I am a card-carrying "circus nut," I asked for a cotton candy machine for Mother's Day one year and my husband bought it for me. My son, David and I were suddenly, weekend concessionaires.

We didn't have a name for our fledgling business. My boys had nicknamed me "Stump" to lovingly poke fun at my short stature. So one day when the tax man came around and asked for our business name and tax number, we grinned at each other and "Stump & Sons" was born.

As time went by, my husband started helping on the weekends. It was so totally different from what he did all week that he really enjoyed it. Upon his suggestion, we added snow cone and popcorn machines that later led to barbecue cookers, a warehouse, etc. and now a full-fledged catering business.

My husband is the public relations man and books the business and events. He only gets involved in the operations part of the business when it is absolutely necessary.

He is the hardest working and most dedicated person in the company, but we all feel he has "delusions of grandeur"! He can never say "no" – no matter how many other functions we may have on a given day. We have scolded and threatened him over and over; but if we have six events scheduled, he is convinced we can handle "just one more"!

This poem is about one of the occasions of overscheduling. We don't know whether to kill him (no jury would convict us) or love him for having so much faith in us. "To kill or not to kill?" That is the question.

MY RICH, THE OPTIMIST!

I cannot believe what we're doing today.
To get it all done, there just ain't no way!!

Here at Stone Mountain, there's a big rodeo.
That's a terrible job and a really big show;

While out at the airfield, we need to be set
For this year's open house – their biggest one yet.

Incidentally, there's also an event at Lanier.
Poe tells them: "No sweat! My crew will be there!"

Tables must be picked up at some rental place.
Just leave it to Poe. "I'll punch in his face!"

We must put up tents – the forecasters are warning.
"But not to worry! They're not needed 'til morning."

The big truck that's vital is not running right,
But it might start tomorrow. "Don't get all uptight!"

We must move the cooker; it wobbles and sways.
It's gonna "jackknife" one of these days.

The truck driver has a patch on one eye.
I try to keep faith, but I'm too young to die.

One son is sick and has to stay home,
And all of our workers are tired to the bone.

But in spite of it all, with God's help we survive
And we sit tired and dirty and try to revive.

While Poe smugly grins and counts all the money
And says to us all: "Want to hear something funny?"

"Everyone was so pleased – I want you to know
Tomorrow I've scheduled a really BIG SHOW!"

FLORENCE NIGHTINGALE, THE LADY WITH THE LAMP

*W*hile I was growing up in a small town in northwest Florida, I had four best friends and we were inseparable. People in town affectionately called us "The Big Five" because we were always together. Even at age sixty-five when I go home, some people still call us that. As we grew up, we shared our dreams of the future and a couple of the girls spoke of becoming nurses. I, however, was not one of them. My usual comment was "YUK!" That profession did not appeal to me at all.

We all graduated from high school together and chose our separate ways. One of these friends and I went off to college together; the others chose other paths. I enrolled in the pharmacy school; but after being there for only ten days, I met my future husband. I passed all my courses that year, but I was hardly what you would call a dedicated student. We became engaged and were married the next June after he graduated from college.

We started a family almost immediately; and thoughts of education, a career, or anything else were put on the "back burner." Three years later, we had two children and they took all my time and energy. I had a miscarriage about this time, and I became very depressed. My self-esteem was practically nil, and I felt trapped and miserable.

When my son was five and my daughter was three, I enrolled in Pensacola Junior College and began my education in YOU GUESSED IT! NURSING. It took three years for me to finish a two-year A.S. degree, but I made it. There were eighty-eight students that began the nursing course with me, and only eleven of that group graduated. I was very proud of myself – as were my family and friends. Even though I was tired and would have preferred to take time off to rest, I decided I needed to go to work immediately to nail down the fundamentals while they were still fresh in my mind.

I have always been a "caretaker," so nursing was a wonderful outlet for me. I fell in love with it immediately and enjoyed it to the fullest.

My biggest problem was learning the difference between "empathy" and "sympathy." I remember the first patient I was ever assigned. He was an old gentleman in his eighties; and he looked so much like my uncle, who had been the closest thing to a grandfather I had ever had, that my first thought was: "I can't do this." It broke my heart to see him in pain.

I went home that afternoon with the full intention of not coming back the next day. As I was crying and driving home, the car radio began to play the song "IF I CAN HELP SOMEBODY ALONG THE WAY, THEN MY LIVING WILL NOT BE IN VAIN." It was as if GOD was speaking directly to me. I knew in my heart that nursing was what GOD wanted for me at this time of my life. I remembered what I had heard that says, "We must do our best, and leave the results to GOD." I soon learned that if I went home each day and worried about my patients all night that I would be no good to them the next day. Still my heart broke at some of the sad situations in which I came in contact. It took time, but I learned to give them the best care I could and then put them in GOD'S HANDS.

I came to realize that nursing was so much more than bed pans, pain medications, and clean sheets. Once I had a patient with terminal cancer, and he was a very young and angry man. He was combative and hostile, and the nurses fought over which one had to care for him. He had dressings that had to be changed, and it was both very painful and embarrassing for him.

One day I came in to work, and they had assigned him to me. With much trepidation, I entered his room and he swore at me. One look in his eyes told me how much pain and fear he was experiencing, and my heart went out to him. I sat down in the chair by his bed, and I told him I could only imagine how angry and afraid he was and that I did not blame him. I explained to him the necessity of keeping his bandages clean and dry and that I would be as careful as I could. I also told him (because from his eyes and anger I could see he felt he had no control over anything anymore): "You are the boss. Tell me the easiest way to do this, and we will do it that way." He seemed to relax; and he began to tell me exactly where to start and what to do, and we did it his way. His way was a little slower than the regular way; but it accomplished the same goal, and he felt like he was allowed some control. When we finished the dressing change, I straightened his bed and gave him his pain medication, and he began to drift off to sleep. Before he slept, he smiled and thanked me for what I had done. He died a few weeks later; but until he did, he demanded that I be his nurse if I was on duty.

One night I was working the dreaded "graveyard" shift from 11 p.m. until 7 a.m. It was reasonably quiet that night, and I made my rounds to check my patients. I always carried a penlight so as not to disturb the patients who were sleeping.

I went into the room of an old black gentleman who never seemed to ask for much. I shined the light toward his bed and saw that he was wide awake – even though it was 3 a.m. I sat down in a chair by his bed and asked if I could do anything for him. He thought a minute and then said, "Yes'um; you can tell me how to die." He had no family, and he was afraid of dying alone. I had the opportunity to witness to him about what I believe. I promised him he would not die alone because GOD loved him and He would be with him every step of the way. The tears ran down his face; and he said, "Thank you, Miss." I held his hand until he fell asleep. The next afternoon when I came to work, GOD had taken him home. I cried, but they were tears of joy because I knew he was not alone or in pain any longer.

Nursing is a noble calling (not a profession). I have been unable to practice nursing (except with my friends and family) for many years because of my disability. It was a heartbreaking blow because I loved my patients, and they loved me. I don't feel my education was wasted because it has helped me in many areas of my life. I would like to think I would still be a good nurse – even at my age. However, I have seen some nurses grow bitter and hard because of low wages and overwork. When a nurse is "burned out," she should change professions; some don't. I have spent a great deal of time in hospitals because of my disability, and it is easy to decide which ones still have their "calling" and those only there for a paycheck.

Like other professions, nursing consists of both good and bad. I have been known, on certain occasions, to suggest to a nurse who doesn't care about her patients that she might want to check into a career at the DOLLAR STORE. It was not usually a popular evaluation, but they got the message. No amount of money can compensate for a loving and caring nurse. The rewards are not monetary; they are the smiles, respect, and gratitude on the faces of the patients and their family. It is being able to go to bed each night and know that you have done something to help another human being in their time of suffering. In some cases, only TINCTURE of TIME can heal a body. Sometimes it will never be healed; but a caring nurse with kind words of encouragement, a tender touch, and a loving smile can help heal the spirit.

Thank You, LORD, for all of the unappreciated, overworked, and underpaid "Ladies with the Lamp" that toil day after day to minister to the needs of their fellowman.

SHATTERED DREAMS

*M*any people can identify with the following poem because they have had dreams and plans for their lives that just did not work out the way they had planned. The shattering of one's dream is very traumatic, and often we feel cheated and despondent because we suffer such disappointment.

We are certain that our plan is the best and the only path our lives should take. It may be many years or we may never know why God chooses a different path for us; but without fail, we realize that God's plan was the better one. Only by blind faith and obedience to God's urging in our lives do we experience and accept the peace that comes from letting God guide us.

SHATTERED DREAMS

In my growing-up years,
I had fantasies and dreams,
Working hard day after day
To achieve my selfish schemes.

Sometimes when we reach our goal,
We think our life is all arranged.
Suddenly things take a turn
That seems unfair and strange.

Dramatically, our life is changed.
Our dreams all fall apart.
All we see with our finite eyes
Are shattered pieces of our heart.

We feel denial, anger, and fear;
For we are not in control.
We suffer disappointment
That reaches to our soul.

Slowly as we stopped the war
We waged day after day,
We felt the comfort of the Lord
As these words we heard HIM say:

"There was nothing wrong with your plan;
It was worthwhile and was good.
But I had a better one in mind,
So you learn the things you should."

GOD'S REMINDER

*S*ome years back, I returned to my hometown to care for my mother who was in the hospital for surgery. I learned early in my nursing career there is a very good reason nurses and doctors cannot treat their own families and close friends. They lose all of their objectivity when the patient is someone they love.

The problem or procedure may be something you have seen or cared for dozens of times; but when the pain or invasion is on the face or the body of someone with whom you have a close relationship, everything changes. You become just another frightened, helpless person, waiting to hear news about your particular loved one.

During this particularly trying time, GOD, in HIS LOVE, gave me a special gift. Right across the hall with her daughter (also a patient) was a close childhood friend with whom I had not spent time in years. We live 350 miles apart. Even though it was a difficult time for us both, we renewed our love and friendship and had a wonderful time catching up with the events of each other's lives.

Since I wrote this poem, my MOM has gone on to her heavenly home. There were five of us girls that went everywhere and did everything together from elementary school through high school. Later, we shared weddings, babies, grandchildren, etc. Everyone in our small hometown knew us affectionately as the "BIG FIVE." At my mother's funeral, all of my four dear friends came to comfort and express their sympathy.

We do not see each other often, but the love and the wonderful memories abide forever. I love you, Carole, Annette, Shirley, and Max. I am grateful GOD put all of you in my life. I also am grateful that our collective parents had the patience of Job.

GOD'S REMINDER

Sometimes when I am burdened and feeling so low,
I wonder why GOD would let it be so.

But each time that it happens, HE gives me a sign
That reminds me I'm HIS and HE is still mine.

This time an old friend, whom I seldom see,
Was HEAVENLY placed to be there with me.

Old tales were retold and memories shared,
And it lifted my spirits to know someone cared.

Years always change things; they can't stay the same;
But our love for each other steadfastly remains.

So thank you, old friend. You made my life brighter
And the ache in my heart a little bit lighter.

MY TURN

*B*ecause of my physical problems, I had many hospitalizations and numerous major surgeries while my children were growing up. My mom was always there to pitch in and help. I always felt safe when she was there. I knew she loved my children as much as I did.

I remember the day we brought our "first-born" son home from the hospital. Neither my husband nor myself had a clue as to how to take care of him. My mom arrived on the train that night. Just as soon as we knew she was there, we all three relaxed – my husband, the baby, and I. The difference in her secure touch – as opposed to our nervous and tentative touch – had a tremendously soothing effect on the baby. All of us, including our baby, knew there was someone there who knew what she was doing.

She was always a great comfort to me. I felt everything would be okay if she were there. My children are all grown now, and my mom has since passed away; but – no matter how old I am – when I get sick, I still want my "MAMA."

I wrote this poem years ago after she had had a heart attack. I saw her in coronary care with all of the tubes and monitors and felt very inadequate that I could not comfort her as she had always comforted me.

MY TURN

So many times she sat by my bed
And held my hand and patted my head.

She'd say, "I'm so sorry that you feel so bad."
Her eyes showed she felt every pain that I had.

She would never complain about my work that she did –
Whether sweeping the floor or washing my kid!

It seemed that somehow she always knew
What would make me feel better when I was blue.

Now she is ill, and it is my turn to care
And worry and suffer with the pain she must bear.

I pray GOD will help me and just let me see
A way I can comfort like she's comforted me.

Please bless my dear mother with THY HEALING TOUCH
And help her feel better because I love her so much!

WAIT AND SEE

The battle against low self-esteem and unworthiness continues to pop up in my life from time to time. It doesn't happen nearly as often as it once did but still often enough to help me remember where I came from and how far I have come.

When I first began to fight this battle, it was a daily, constant struggle. I used every trick in the book to avoid being alone and having to face myself and my fears.

With God's help, I have been able to face my fear and learn that I am not all bad – neither am I all good but a human mixture who God can love and accept unconditionally just as I am. This does not mean God will not continue to put lessons in my path to help me grow but that, wherever I happen to be on my path, He loves and accepts me and provides for my needs.

These lessons are painful; and many times, if I had a choice, I would avoid them. However, God's plan does not allow this. The same lesson will be placed in my path – in one form or another – until I finally learn what God is trying to teach me. Each lesson makes me more like God and helps me love and accept myself and others more easily.

WAIT AND SEE

For so very many years,
There was a place I'd never be.
I didn't want to be alone
With no one else but me.

The TV and the radio
I never did turn down.
I didn't want to know myself
For fear of what I found.

Then one day – even through my fear,
My Father said to me,
"Trust Me, child. You have to look
If indeed you would be free."

So with God's help – very timidly,
I dared to take a peek.
Yes, there was a lot to throw away
But also lots to keep.

There's good and bad in all of us;
God made us all that way;
But what is bad and what is good
Only God can say.

But if we become as children
And let God have His way;
He will make a lovely vessel
From our ugly lump of clay.

Then we won't have to hide again
Or fear what we might be
'Cause we will learn to love ourselves
As God does. Wait and see!!

ANNIVERSARY LETTER

June 9, 1994

My Darling Children,

Today is our 40th wedding anniversary. In this day and age, your father and I feel almost like an endangered species because we are still married but more than that (since some couples stay together out of fear, peer pressure, for their children, etc.) because we are still in love. I thought I loved him when we were married in 1954, but that was so "pale" compared to now. Now we are two halves of the same person. The Bible says, "Cleave together, and the twain shall become one." This is so true.

Please be patient with my ramblings; but I feel I have to tell you about this wonderful man and the beautiful gift I have given each of you by marrying that 128-pound "Tiger" on June 9, 1954. We were so young (me barely 19 and he only 21). Can you believe I was still growing (no comment!)? I am an inch taller now than then. He had already finished college and his four years in the Navy. He was already quite the "deal maker" because he had acquired a VA loan; and we moved into what we thought was the most beautiful, little two-bedroom house ever six weeks after we were married. He didn't believe in rent. We bought appliances with payments of $39, furniture with a $33-a-month payment, a $54 car payment, a $56-a-month house payment, $11-a-month payments on my rings, etc. Both sets of parents said it couldn't be done since your dad made $250 a month and I made $175 a month working as a secretary at Howard College. I soon became pregnant (which was our fondest dream) and had problems and had to quit work soon, leaving us with only one salary.

One of my fondest memories is an occasion when we had twenty-five cents between us. I was still working at the time and was pregnant with Dave. Your dad gave me the quarter because back then you could get a bowl of soup and crackers at the cafeteria for twenty-five cents. While he was in the shower, I slipped it in his pocket so he would have coffee money. At noon, when I was out walking to pass my lunch hour, he drove up (probably fifteen miles round trip) to bring me the quarter. He said, "There are two of you who need to eat!"

Had I known how precious that act was, I would have skipped the soup and preserved the quarter.

Our living room and dining room had matching plastic curtains (ninety-nine cents a pair); but to us, they were beautiful. Back then a new mattress was rounded at first until you slept on it a few nights. For the first few nights, we had to hold on to each other to keep from falling off and that's what this letter is about – the man God gave me to hold onto to keep from falling off.

I don't think I have to tell any of you what a kind, loving, and generous man my husband is; but I think every decade or so I need to tell you how much he means to me and how much I admire and respect him. You all know I love him; I want to tell you why!

He is kind and generous to a fault. He is sensitive to everything around him. He is patient and unselfish and tries to help anyone he sees or hears of in need. He is very strong in a gentle way that earns him love and respect without demanding it. He is ambitious and talented, but his ambitions are not selfish in nature. He wants success for everyone around him. He has a wonderful sense of humor and is able to laugh at himself as loudly as anyone around him. He loves his family, people in general, and life. He believes in his fellowman – no matter how many times they let him down!! He is a Christian and tries to live his creed every day, not just on Sunday. Christian principles stream through his eyes and his life every day.

However, the characteristic that has meant the most to me is his POSITIVE attitude. No matter what happens, he believes in the future and assumes things will get better. It is this part of his character that has kept me from "falling off" so many times.

We both get somewhat upset when people are so shocked that we still have a "happy" marriage. They tell us how "lucky" we are. We are quick to say that "luck" had nothing to do with it. Mutual respect, communication, courtesy, thoughtfulness, and genuine hard work are the keys. It's worth the effort!

There have been many hard times over the years when it might have been easier to "throw in the towel"; but thank God, we didn't. There were times when we didn't agree on things or we had money problems or we just plain didn't like each other that we could have rationalized going our separate ways, but "for better or worse" meant just that to us. We really considered nothing else.

If I had to sum up the secret to our happy marriage, it would be this: We have given each other respect and room to grow. We have realized that by each having his private thoughts, dreams, and experiences we can keep from growing "stale." We are not jealous! A marriage without trust is worthless and miserable. By allowing each other our own space, we can bring fresh, new ideas and experiences to our mutually shared lives. Neither of us would have made it with a jealous or "smothering" partner who stunted our growth. Rich is my closest friend but not my ONLY friend, and the same is true for him. We both need other people and time away from each other.

He is my "touchstone." My life is nailed down in him. No matter what happens, he is my "snug harbor" where I am loved and protected. I can wander away and do my thing; but like a lighthouse, his love, comfort, and understanding are always there for me to lead me safely through the rough channels. Oh, he still has his annoying habits; and he isn't perfect. What would I do with a PERFECT man? I'm not perfect, and he tolerates my annoying habits and loves me anyway. When I was ill for so long, he made me feel loved, cherished, needed, and worthwhile – even when I knew what a burden I must have been.

Rich said to me recently, "Have I told you lately how much I love you?" (He is very loving and affectionate, and I have a tendency to take all this for granted.) This certain day I was more sensitive to his question and realized how fortunate I was to have such a question asked and I replied, "Yes, my darling, every day since I've known you and not just in cheap words but in actions that count." It is wonderful to live and love with someone who still sees me as his nineteen-year old bride of forty years ago.

I am indeed a fortunate and blessed lady because I have enjoyed the love of the best parents, the best husband, the best children, the best grandchildren, and the best friends; and I thank God for all my blessings. On this 40th anniversary, I realize what the poet meant when he wrote: "GROW OLD WITH ME. THE BEST IS YET TO BE!"

Love,

Mom

WHICH POWER?

*W*e are in the catering and concession business. For awhile, we did catering and concessions at Lake Lanier Islands until we decided it was too far to drive to be worthwhile. We still cater some larger parties up there but not on a regular basis as before.

If you have ever been there, you know the scenery is breathtaking. There is a lot of water and beautiful trees; and the landscape is perfect with its well-manicured shrubs and beautiful flower beds.

One day – even with God's wonder all around me, it was a particularly aggravating and exasperating day. I couldn't seem to get my "attitude" anywhere near where it should be. Finally, someone suggested rather strongly that I take my "attitude" and go for a walk before I killed somebody.

I took their advice and went walking. Finally, I wandered down by the edge of the lake to try to collect my frazzled nerves. I sat down on a rock and let my mind drift. As usual, when I am still and receptive, God speaks to me. Very soon, my anger and self-pity were taken away and replaced by a new patience and a real sense of gratitude, remembering that God has no clock and I can start my day over anytime.

WHICH POWER?

Lately, it seems my life is bogged down
In the quicksand of ego and fear.
My heart seems so fastened to the world and its cares –
I forget that MY FATHER is near!

But today a wise friend said, "Just look at yourself.
Can't you see what a mess you are making?
Just go talk to GOD and LISTEN to HIM.
He'll show you the wrong turns you are taking."

So I found a quiet spot near a beautiful lake
Where God's handiwork was easy to see.
With each lap of a wave, my body relaxed
And God's voice began speaking to me:

"Do you see that boat that those people are rowing
And struggling so hard to control?
They are so tired and full of despair
'Cause they want to own their own soul!

"Now look at the boat with the power to spare
That comes from a source from without.
They're laughing and happy – not struggling at all –
'Cause their power never gives out.

"You have a choice of which power to use:
MY POWER or oars of your making.
Why do you forget to ask for this power
When it's always there for the taking?"

Then I glanced up at a dogwood tree,
And my heart was instantly touched.
Legend has it this tree made the cross.
MY GOD! HE LOVED ME SO MUCH!!!

If YOU gave YOUR SON to die in my place,
Is it not the least I can do
To believe YOU'LL protect me and all those I love.
Every day YOU prove that it's true!

So God help me be willing to trust YOU enough
To live every day without fear.
Please help me "LET GO" and give me the PEACE
That comes from knowing YOU'RE near!!!

HE LIKES ME

*A*s I grow older, I learn more and more about what is really important in life. My shallow, superficial values are replaced by an understanding of the deeper, more spiritual things. They are not temporal things that don't last but insights God gives me that will stay with me forever.

I had a happy and beautiful marriage for nearly fifty years with a man handpicked for me by GOD HIMSELF. Our relationship was based on a mutual love, trust, and respect that grew with each passing day.

What I thought love to be in the early years of our marriage pales in comparison to what I now feel for the wonderful, kind, and gentle man GOD chose for me. The original lust that is so overwhelming in the beginning of a relationship slowly turns to a much deeper and more comfortable feeling that culminates into a union of two kindred spirits whose thoughts, actions, and experiences ebb and flow from one heart to another. This bond, carefully worked and not neglected, grows deeper and more beautiful every day – much like a well-tended garden.

I never had any reason to doubt my husband's love. He was thoughtful and affectionate and missed only a handful of days telling me how loved and appreciated I was.

I am ashamed to admit that at times I took his love and caring for granted. I was always caught short when I realized that many women do not have a clue as to what it would be like to be married to such a man.

I depended on his love a great deal; but it was a really special moment when one day I realized not only did he love me, but he also LIKED me. Because of our wedding vows, LOVE is mandatory but LIKING is optional. I indeed felt blessed to have both.

HE LIKES ME

We have been married
For nearly fifty years.
There were so many good times
Sprinkled with tears.

We have been given the good times,
But GOD wants us to know
That our tears are the moisture
That helps us to grow.

Our babies are grown;
They are out of the house.
Sometimes we just sit here
As quiet as a mouse.

But I know he is here;
He knows I am too.
And there's not a thing
That we wouldn't do

To cling to each other –
Come whatever might –
And to help one another.
The whole world we would fight.

We miss all the children;
They all have our love.
But this time in our lives
Is a gift from above.

The young man I married
Is still my best "BEAU."
Like me, he has faults;
But I still love him so.

Last Sunday morning –
As we lay in our bed,
His arm was around me.
He was stroking my head.

He looked in my eyes.
His nice smile just spread.
His words were the sweetest
He ever had said:

"I really do like you."
My heart skipped a beat.
"I like you too!"
I heard my voice repeat.

I've loved many people
Because I felt that I should;
But if I didn't have to,
I don't think that I would.

I wish them all well,
But that's where it ends.
Because I didn't like them,
We were never real friends.

He has to "LOVE" me;
He promised he would.
But to say that he "LIKED" me
Made me feel special and good.

So thank GOD for the cake –
I pray "LOVE" never ends –
But much more for the frosting
Because "LIKE" makes us friends.

MY BEST

I never thought of myself as a controlling person; but as I have taken an honest inventory of myself, I can see that control is a definite character defect of mine. Even though I was gracious and kind and used "velvet glove" manipulation, I was always seeking to satisfy my self-centered need to be in control.

As I have grown emotionally and spiritually, I realize that control of anything or anybody, including myself, is an illusion and is not real. Once I get past the illusion to the reality, I realize I am powerless! Amazingly, it is only when I admit my powerlessness that I ever gain any control in my life.

I have "selective amnesia," and this principle of powerlessness is one of the most difficult for me to remember. If I do my ten percent, God will gladly take care of the rest. It is such a freeing experience when I do remember – and it has never, ever failed. Why do I have so much trouble remembering it??

MY BEST

I have a few problems to deal with today.
I must choose how I handle them in my own way!

People around me don't know how I feel.
But to me, they're important; to me, they're quite real.

Like a child in the dark who fears the unknown,
My life has it shadows – no matter I'm grown.

Everyone has his own set of problems to bear,
And we struggle each day with trouble and care.

Sometimes we feel we don't have the right
To impose all our problems on the people we might.

So we muddle along – our hearts aching with strain,
Trying to cope with our grief and our pain.

We tell ourselves, "We're doing our best";
But how well are we doing? That is the test.

Is it our best to keep fighting each day;
Or is there a much better, easier way?

Do we have to handle things and be in control
Or call on the ONE who's THE LORD OF OUR SOUL?

Life is so easy when we give HIM the reins
And avoid all the struggle with life and its strains.

We feel only a coward gives his problems away.
A brave man just copes with them day after day.

I'm sure in God's plan His greatest task
Was to teach finite man he had only to ask

And a joy and a peace would enter his life
That would help him to deal with the stress and the strife.

Our best always means we don't do it alone.
We remember OUR FATHER on His heavenly throne.

And like a tired child who has broken his toys,
Someone wiser must fix them and give back our joys.

So when your heart is breaking, remember the test:
You do your part, and give God all the rest.

THE CIRCLE OF LIFE

*N*ext month I will celebrate my sixty-fifth birthday. Admittedly, it will not be as traumatic for me as for some of my friends. At sixty-five, it is fairly depressing to sign up for Social Security and Medicare. I escaped this trauma because I have been on Social Security disability and Medicare since 1977. It is still a milestone because that is officially the age when EVERYONE considers you a senior citizen.

When I was ten or so years of age, I was certain that, if by some miracle, a person ever reached that age, he would be a mindless, drooling shell of a human being. Even though – with some of my health problems – I have short periods of self-pity and depression, for the most part, I realize that in many ways each stage of my life is better than the last. For every aspect of our life that deteriorates, GOD seems to find a new and exciting one to compensate. It is abundantly clear to me that GOD has a DIVINE PLAN for each of us. Even though we do not understand it, it is nonetheless HIS DIVINE PLAN.

I always thought it was interesting that GOD had such an INCREDIBLE SENSE OF HUMOR – that the first twelve-step program, Krispy Kreme Donuts, and I should all be born in the same year. In my finite mind, it proves that GOD knew I would need both to cope with and enrich my life.

There have been many radical changes in my lifetime. I can remember outhouses, ice from iceboxes that weren't electric, kerosene lamps, the first naked light bulbs hanging down from the ceiling. I remember baths in a tub near the heater that heated the only warm room in the whole house, and I can still feel the tons of quilts that covered me in an unheated bedroom. I remember the whole family going to bed early.

My dad would put the radio in a central location; so we could all listen to LUX RADIO, EDGAR BERGEN, FIBBER MCGEE AND MOLLY, MR. DISTRICT ATTORNEY, and so many other wonderful talents. These stars

– like RED SKELTON, for example – believed it was their duty to entertain while reinforcing family values and patriotism. They used four-letter words like LOVE, CARE, HELP, etc. and made us laugh at ourselves from a happiness down deep in our souls that was evoked from our own experiences or those of our neighbors. Sometimes we cried with empathy for our fellowman's suffering. These feelings were not "jerked out" by violence and gore and mind-boggling filth and cruelty – like our grandchildren are exposed to today.

I remember when as children we were sent out to play and entertain ourselves with our own imaginations. MARIO BROTHERS ran the Italian market on the corner. Everyone believed in GOD; and if they didn't, they kept it very quiet. Boys fell in love with girls; and men married women and raised GOD-FEARING, obedient children. Of course, children still got in trouble; and sometimes it was serious; but it was not because parents were so apathetic or preoccupied that they turned over the responsibility for their child's sense of values to the church, the school, or anyone else who would accept it.

I am only too aware of how times have changed and the pressures that today's parents and children have to bear. Gratefully, mine was an easier time. No one felt obliged to lock doors, have car alarms, security systems, more than one or two law enforcement officers in town, drug tests, lie detectors for employment, and so many other things that are now accepted as common practice. The only guns around were hunting rifles, and a DRUG DEALER was the local pharmacist.

When I compare the new with the old, I sometimes get very discouraged and I lament that things were never so bad and I have to believe this is true. However, I imagine if we talked with the pioneers who had no modern machines, conveniences, or technology and who were in constant dread of Indians inflicting the first form of MALE-PATTERN BALDNESS, we might get a pretty convincing argument.

Sometimes when I am discouraged and can see no rhyme or reason to this whole dilemma, GOD sends me a glimmer of understanding that only reminds me of the verse in the BIBLE that says, "Now I see through a glass, darkly, but then face to face." This verse taps me on the shoulder and says, "HOW MANY TIMES DO I HAVE TO TELL YOU THAT I KNOW WHAT I AM DOING, AND WHERE DOES IT SAY YOU HAVE TO UNDERSTAND?" It is a humbling reminder; and when I accept it is none of my business and go on doing what I feel is the "NEXT RIGHT THING," GOD gives me that little glimmer. This glimmer is actually what this piece is about.

A year or so ago, my husband and I took two of our grandchildren to see "The Lion King." It was a delightful, little Disney production. It was the story of a great and wise lion who was the ruler of the jungle and the birth of his son, the prince, who would be the new ruler when he grew up. In essence, it was the story of THE CIRCLE OF LIFE. It dealt with the concept of the "food chain" and how one day you would be at the top, and later you will circle around and be at the bottom. During the span of the movie, we witnessed the evolving of a strong king through the misadventures and trials endured while seeking to accept his place as the new king after the death of his father. Only by remembrance of his father's words and the things he had been taught by him was he able to find his way on his journey back to his rightful place as ruler. His journey involved many trials that seemed painful and unnecessary, but only through these trials was he able to become strong enough to succeed in his quest and overcome his difficulties. At the end of the movie, the new king was introducing HIS newborn son to his loving subjects. The movie ended at this point, but even the children in the audience realized this process would repeat itself over and over again.

I have seen this same circle happening in my own family. When my younger son was eleven or twelve years of age, his maternal grandfather would load him in his Volkswagen camper every summer and they would take off for two or three weeks. Usually they headed out west to Yellowstone National Park – among many other places they visited. My dad taught him so many things on those trips. Even more than the different cultures, geography, mores, wildlife, and camping skills, he learned values and heard family history and saw first-hand what it was like to be both a "tough" and a "gentle" man. He heard his grandfather pray and read the Bible, and my dad showed him where he stood with GOD. He learned to appreciate that this man stood for certain things and that, most of all, he was one on which my son could depend. He made a young boy in his formative years feel special and appreciated and assured that he could be anything he wanted to be if he was willing to work for it. Mainly, he learned you get out of life about what you put in it. A few years back, my now thirty-five-year-old son told me if he could relive any period in his life, it would be the time that he and his GRAN GRAN spent together.

What does this have to do with the subject? I'm getting to that. My son has since been transferred; but at this particular time, he was a salesman and traveled in and out of northwest Florida where my dad still lives. He will be ninety-four next month – although you would never know it. One day my son called his grandfather from Mobile, Alabama; went though Milton, Florida where my dad lives; picked him up and took him to Panama City, Florida to make sales calls and to install one of the communication systems he sold. They called me that night after they returned to my dad's home, and they had had a wonderful time. My dad had to tell me about watching my son install the system, and I could hear the pride in his voice. Tears came to my eyes as I hung up the phone. Once again, GOD had given me a glimpse of THE CIRCLE OF LIFE.

Now the child was taking care of the man, and it was a beautiful concept that only GOD could have designed. When I see GOD'S HAND in something so beautiful and practical, HOW COULD I EVER DOUBT GOD'S LOVE OR WISDOM?

CHILDREN

*M*y older son is the father of a wonderful nine-year-old daughter and a precious seven-year-old son. He is a great dad, and I am very proud of his parenting ability. His children think he is the original "moonhanger," and they really enjoy their time with him. He plays with them and takes them to work with him occasionally. He prays with them; and they have a "Secret Club" where they discuss all their thoughts, concerns, and plans. Most of the time, it is reasonably tranquil when the three of them are together; but once in a while (like yesterday), things became a little "rocky."

It was a raw and rainy day, and Dad was not feeling well. In spite of this, he picked them up early from after-school care. He had taken his son to karate, and he had gotten them a treat; but still they were whining and unhappy because they wanted to go skating that evening. We both tried to reason with them, but they still insisted that no one ever did ANYTHING for THEM. We reminded them of all the nice things we all do, but they were in the proverbial "What have you done for me for me lately?" mode.

Parenting is the singularly most important job in the world. For this position, we, without a doubt, receive the least preparation or instruction. We must have a license to drive, to get married, and to indulge in most businesses or professions. Heck, we even have to have a license to yank a fish out of the water; but even youngsters, who are still babies themselves, can have parenthood thrust upon them. They don't have a clue what it is all about. Sadly, however, age and affluence don't automatically qualify one anymore than the youngsters.

I can remember people telling me before our first child was born: "Don't worry. Maternal instinct kicks in, and you just do what comes naturally!" What a joke!

This totally self-centered, little tyrant arrives; and your lives are never you're own or the same again. How something so small and totally dependent on someone else for everything can take up so much time, energy, and space is remarkable. There are exceptions to his dependency, however; that is, when to spit up on your best outfit or have bodily functions occur – with their foul smells – at the most inopportune moments. Certain times are understood: (1) at the photographer; (2) on a short trip when he is alone in the car with you and you are already late for an appointment; (3) when you have just finished bathing and dressing him; (4) any occasion when someone you want to impress with the fact that you have the cutest, most wonderful baby ever born (especially if they have no children and are uncomfortable around babies anyway) is involved.

You no longer have any private or recreation time. You are always exhausted because of their constant demands at all hours of the day or night. Your personal hygiene consists of dabbing at yourself with a baby wipe if there is time. Your uniform is a flannel nightgown because you never have a chance to change, and a sex life is something you promise you will never take a chance on again. You learn very quickly to heat a bottle with one hand while carrying your "Lord and Master" on your opposite hip. Experts don't agree with me, but I think babies have these devious little personalities that conceive all of these seemingly random acts to drive you insane.

My first child made me "nuts" because I was afraid to touch him. My husband was eager to help; but being an only child himself, he wasn't much of an authority either. The baby cried constantly until my mom arrived. She held him with a confident touch and made him feel safe – something we did not do.

Just as you are ready to put them out with the garbage, you pick them up and rock them and they finally go to sleep. As you look down at them, you could swear that only an angel could be that sweet and beautiful and you are HOOKED! There is nothing in the world more awe inspiring than rocking a baby to sleep and realizing how much he must trust you to feel comfortable enough to let go and fall asleep in your arms. When my first grandchild was born, I made a sampler for her nursery wall that said, "Go away cobwebs. Dust go to sleep. I'm rocking my baby 'cause babies don't keep."

My first child is in his forties, and it seems like only yesterday he was a baby. I can remember all of his firsts and picture them in my mind. I remember the first time he laughed out loud. I was so thrilled that I almost made him throw up trying to get him to do it over and over. There is no more delightful sound in the world than a baby's laughter. When a baby is clean and warm and you kiss their neck, their odor – mixed with the smell of baby powder – is much more fragrant and priceless than the most expensive man-made perfume.

Being a parent is hard work; but when your child snuggles up close to you and tells you, "Mommy, I love you"; there is no feeling in the world that will melt your heart and make you feel so needed and immortal. During these magic moments, we realize that no matter how devious, how demanding, and infuriating they may be, they are GOD'S GREATEST GIFTS to us and we would gladly lay down our lives for them without question if it became necessary.

Parenthood taught me the meaning of unconditional love. It made me know there is nothing my child could do that would make me stop loving him. It was a vivid lesson of GOD'S UNCONDITIONAL LOVE for us.

Being a parent to me is one of GOD'S greatest teaching implements. When I am honestly seeking a more personal relationship with GOD, I receive all kinds of object lessons. I see my children and grandchildren as being self-centered (just like me). I see them act without considering the consequences (just like me). I see them being thoughtless and selfish and hurting others (just like me). I see them frustrated when they can't control things (just like me). I see them insist on their own way and make mistakes that hurt them (just like me). I see them regret their actions and have to admit they were wrong and ask for forgiveness (just like me). I see their earthly father take them in his arms and tell them how much they are loved and that they are forgiven (just like me)!

Thank You, FATHER, for the wonderful gift of children who teach us what

You meant when You said, "Suffer the little children to come unto me and forbid them not, for such is the KINGDOM OF HEAVEN." By observing children, we can learn about the carefree spirit that comes from faith and absolute trust – that their father will take care of them. Give us what we need in order not to break that trust. This kind of trust will enable them to understand GOD'S LOVE more easily.

Help us to remember that in the world our children face on a daily basis is a world with much violence and little spirituality. They encounter it on TV as well as many other sources. Let our spirituality and our relationship with YOU be strong enough to shine through to them. The old adage says, "What you do speaks so loud I can't hear what you are saying."

Bless us with the love and patience to be kind, respectful, and as patient with them as YOU are with us. Let us stop to think before we speak or act and try to see our children through YOUR EYES. Make our homes a place of peace and understanding so that our children always feel safe there. Help us not to stomp on the tender roots of their souls anymore than we would stomp on the tender shoots of a young plant.

We know these children are not our own but gifts loaned to us. Give them happy memories, and instill in them their importance in YOUR PLAN. Never let us forget how important we are in our children's lives and remember how short the time is when we are allowed to be the most important people in their world. Parents are always needed but never as much as when they are young and learning about a parent-child relationship. If children believe their earthly father loves them unconditionally, it is much easier for them to believe their HEAVENLY FATHER does too.

TO BREAK OR TO FIX IT –
THAT IS THE QUESTION

*A*s I have mentioned, I suffer quite a bit with neck pain. I am on several anti- inflammatory medications, but in 1990 my internist decided that physical therapy might make my pain more bearable.

Enter DON CROCHET. Little did I know that the ink was not yet dry on his diploma and his license was "in the mail." He was very professional and properly impressed with my "blue-haired, old lady routine." I think back and decide it was a draw as to which "hood winked" the other the most that day.

To make this story short, I will say only that he has held me together with "DUCT TAPE" for the last almost thirteen years. Little did I know that this young, tall, skinny kid would become one of the best friends I have had in my life. He continues to work on my neck; he has worked on my feet; he went to surgery with me when I had my knee replaced; he did the PT after my shoulder surgery; and now we are dealing with my back.

Often I will overhear him saying to another patient, "I think you are ready to be discharged" after six weeks or so. Laughingly, I ask, "When are you going to say that to me?" He replies, "Not in this lifetime." Every once in awhile, I decide I don't really need to go; but my neck seems to know when it is Thursday (my regular appointment day), and it convinces me that maybe I should go a while longer. Besides I would miss him and I hope he would miss me if I didn't keep coming.

We are family now. I know his wife; his two boys call me "Grammy Gay"; and he was right there to comfort me when my husband passed away. I know I can depend on him; I even had Easter dinner at his home this year.

God has put many wonderful people in my life, but I will always consider Don a very special one. This silly little poem is a tribute to my Don. Thanks Pal!

TO BREAK OR TO FIX IT - THAT IS THE QUESTION

I've always had trouble with my short, little neck.
I must remember to treat it with the utmost respect.

Many doctors and tortures I have undergone.
They shake their heads saying, "We can't fix what is wrong."

Surgeries, needles, and pills by the gross.
Guess they're all useful but what helps me the most

Is a "stringbean" named "Don" who'll pull and then crack
And gets all his assistants into the act.

I dress in a gown that's really quite fetching.
Say you saw it in "Vogue," and the truth you'd be stretching.

First they wrap me in hot packs they pick up with tongs.
"Now don't you worry! They'll cool off before long."

They place cold, wet electrodes on my body with care.
They turn on the juice, and they whisper a prayer.

When I don't "sizzle," they relax – oh, so charitable:
"Please let us know when the pain is UNBEARABLE!"

When my pulse rate slows down and I stop my wheezing,
They pour "gook" on my back I know they've been freezing.

Bracing their feet up on the wall,
They "elbow" my sore spots and give it their all.

When "Igor" and "Morticia" have no strength left to burn,
Dr. Frankenstein enters – he lives for his turn.

As his model patient, I always do what I'm told;
But at every visit, he feels he has to scold.

Just a helpless, ole blue hair, I never cause trouble.
Anything he suggests, I do on the double.

Sometimes when his hands are wrapped round my neck,
I have this feeling his thoughts are suspect.

After the ice, I might give him some grief;
But to my surprise, I've gotten relief.

I guess to be truthful, I can be quite a pest.
I can whimper and whine right up there with the best.

But my "Don" is kind, patient, and giving;
And without all his help, I'm not sure I'd be living.

MY MAMA PASSED THE TEST

*M*y mother left this earth on October 7, 1993 at the age of eighty-nine. She had lived a full life before she became ill, and then she suffered for a long time. She was a very proud and independent lady, and it was very hard for her to accept that she could not continue to do all the things she wanted to do and that she had always done. She became dependent on others, and it was particularly difficult for her. As I advance in years and have more and more ailments, I, too, have become more limited in what I can do. Like my mother, I don't accept help gracefully.

I loved my mother very much, and she loved me; but sometimes she could be difficult – as I'm sure I am at times. My physical problems kept me from visiting her as often as I would have liked; and even though it couldn't be helped, I felt guilty. I wrote the following eulogy in her memory because I felt it was the last thing I could do for her:

This is not a day for tears and sadness. This is the day that the LORD hath made, and we should rejoice and be glad in it. This is a day of celebration! My mother's long, hard journey has finally come to an end; and she is resting in the ARMS OF JESUS. She has no more pain and no more tears. She is having a reunion with all the loved ones and friends that have gone on before her, and she has the PEACE THAT PASSETH UNDERSTANDING.

As most of you who knew her know, she sometimes appeared abrasive and gruff; but if you didn't let her scare you away, you came to realize that underneath that "tough" façade was a loving and caring woman who basically wished everyone well. The more she loved you, the more she tested you and picked on you.

Mother liked to tell the story of the night I was born. She said we both stayed awake all night and looked at each other. I liked to kid her and say, "Yes, ma'am! From the first time I laid eyes on you, I knew you would bear watching!"

She picked at me all my life. I used to call her "The East Coast Distributor for

Guilt." She wore her feelings on her sleeve. She could dish it out, but she could-n't take it very well. I used to always walk out of a store before she checked out because I knew she would get in an argument before she got out. Even though the population of Milton had more than quadrupled in the time she lived there, she still couldn't understand how anyone could have the audacity to ask her for iden-tification to cash a check. After all, she had lived here seventy years.

This was the only side that many people saw, and they were very intimidated by her. It's true, you never had to wonder where you stood or what she thought about anything. As those of you who persevered found out – that even though she would never make the "diplomatic service," there was another soft, loving, and sweet-spirited side of her that was even more real than the façade she tried to hide behind.

Parts of her childhood and her younger life were very sad and hard. She lived through the "Great Depression" – with all the fear that entailed. She was a hard worker. I can remember when I was a child that she got us up and fed us and made us ready for school, made the beds, washed the dishes, and had the evening meal on cooking before she left to be at work at 8 a.m. All this she did after she had already cooked my dad's breakfast and gotten him off to work.

This is the side of her that washed and ironed and sacrificed for her family and put cardboard into her own shoe, so we could have a new pair. This part nursed us when we were sick, read the Bible to us, and prayed for us, and saw that we were in church every Sunday.

This is also the side I treasure so much because it allowed her to love and be faith-ful to one man for over sixty-five years (granted that love was usually expressed at the top of their voices). I didn't understand their brand of love for a long time; but it finally began to sink in when one day I took up for one of them and they both jumped on me.

This side of her was always around after I was married and had surgery and phys-ical problems. These situations brought her to my house where she cared for us or brought my children to her house where she cared for them for months at a time when I was not able physically to do it. My children and all her grandchildren loved her very much and had many fun times with her.

This side visited shut-ins, taught a Primary Sunday school class, was interrupted at all times of the day and night (mostly at meal times) to write a check for someone at the church, visited nursing homes, made phone calls to check on the sick, cooked cakes and other things for sick people just because she loved them but did not always know how to say it.

This side also believed that JESUS died for her sins and that HE could always be found at THE FIRST BAPTIST CHURCH OF MILTON, FLORIDA where she and so many of her friends and loved ones found HIM. My mother was a blessed lady and was loved by many. GOD BLESS YOU, Ma! We will miss you.

I wrote the following poem on her birthday, five days before her death.

MY MAMA PASSED THE TEST

When I was just a little girl
And in my bed at night,
One thought kept coming back to me.
It shook my soul with fright.

That thought was of my parents.
What would happen if they died?
I could not live without them
I felt down deep inside.

As I grew older and I learned
How seasons come and go,
I began to see GOD'S plan
And my faith began to grow.

Even if we grow quite old
Through days both right and wrong,
We use this life for practice
To sing GOD'S HEAVENLY SONG.

Babies are born; people die;
The circle goes around.
Both the sad things and the glad things
Are "growth" things we have found.

It was my Mama's birthday.
I knew it was her last.
Her usefulness on this earth
Was truly in the past.

I felt she saw the other side
Where her loved ones for her wait
To share with her the wonder
As she comes through Heaven's Gate.

Death that seemed so very cruel –
When I used to worry so –
Is now a friend that takes you in
Where no tears or pain you'll know.

You had your faults like we all do;
But you passed every test
Because when it came to a mother's love,
You gave your very best.

GOD'S THANKSGIVING

*T*oday is Thanksgiving Day 1993, and I have blessings too numerous to mention. God has been so good to me and my family that – even though I am supposed to be a writer – I don't have the words to describe how full my heart is today.

It is hard to describe my feelings. My mother died last month, and this is our first holiday without her. When some person has been there ever since you took your first breath, it is very strange and sad to think about the fact that you will never see them on this earth again. At first, it is like a dream and you feel as if you will wake up and it won't be real; but slowly you face reality and learn to accept it.

However, since I have grown spiritually, even this sadness is replaced with the knowledge that this, too, is a part of God's plan and cycle and that only through death can we have life eternal. Now as those I love pass on, I realize this is just another stepping stone on our journey to a land where there is no pain, no tears, and no separation from those we love. This place is something that we cannot imagine with our finite minds because it was designed by our loving Heavenly Father. He has pulled out all the stops because we are his children.

As I have mentioned before, DEATH – that was once so frightening to me as a child – is now more of a friend. It takes us away from our place of trials and tears to a place of peace and everlasting serenity.

Today, dear Father, I thank You for this new awareness I have learned that one of our greatest blessings is knowing in Your time we will step through the door of death to the beautiful place YOU YOURSELF have designed for us. You love us unconditionally and choose to give us MERCY instead of JUSTICE.

GOD'S THANKSGIVING

There is one more face missing
At our table today
Because my loving mother
Has just passed away.

She's feasting with all
That before her have gone –
As they sit at GOD'S TABLE
At the foot of HIS THRONE.

Like the others who've gone,
We still miss as before;
And we feel any minute
She'll walk in the door.

Young, new faces replace
The tired and the old;
But our memories linger.
They are as precious as gold.

I long for the day
When we will all be a part
Of GOD'S THANKSGIVING FEAST
That we know in our heart.

GOD has prepared us a home
That is part of HIS PLAN.
The real Feast is HIS LOVE
In HIS OWN NAIL-SCARRED hand.

We will be happy –
No tears, never sad.
HE'LL forgive our mistakes –
No matter how bad.

And all of those faces
We are longing to see
Will be part of heaven
For you and for me.

THANKSGIVING

I t is hard to believe that another year is almost gone. The Olympics that seemed so far in the future when first announced have come and gone. Children whom I remember as four or five year olds are marrying and having children of their own. People whom I loved and admired have died; and my wrinkles, aches, and pains have increased.

This is the time of year when we are making plans for our THANKSGIVING CELEBRATIONS. We are having the usual dysfunctional family discussions about where we will spend Thanksgiving, who will be there, what goodies will be served, sleeping arrangements, and all the other decisions with which we struggle each year. By the time Thanksgiving dinner is over, we are all worn out and already dreading CHRISTMAS when we do it all again.

In fantasy, I am transported to a simpler time when the holiday called Thanksgiving began. A group that wanted religious freedom so badly was willing to risk their lives and leave their homes and extended families to sail from their homeland (definitely not on a luxury liner) to a new uncharted wilderness. There were absolutely no creature comforts when they arrived, and many of those who managed to survive the voyage did not survive their first winter in this land. By sheer will and their faith in GOD, some of these courageous people managed to build crude homes and planted limited crops to survive. Because of their faith and determination, they managed to survive a whole year enduring these hardships. They were still uncomfortable but free; and their hearts were filled with gratitude to the point that they wanted to come together in celebration of life, freedom, and the blessings GOD had bestowed upon them.

The Indians (the Native Americans) watched from a distance the arrival of these strange white people and saw how hard they worked and the sacrifices they made to endure. When the Thanksgiving celebration began, the Indians came into the settlement and brought food that they had to add to the scanty feast. The REDMAN and the WHITEMAN sat together and offered thanks for the blessings they had received during this first, almost unbearable year. There were no congressional edicts or Civil Rights Movements to make these people integrate. There was only friendship and survival and thanksgiving, and it was truly a celebration of life and thankfulness.

Back to today – instead of trying to keep things simple and enjoying our blessings with our families and friends, we rush around being sure that everyone's favorite dish is available so that we are totally exhausted and can't wait for everyone to go home, so we can rest. Except for the grace that is said before dinner, there is little time or inclination to spend on really considering all of the blessings we have enjoyed our whole lives (not just this year). The things we take so for granted were not even things that the first Thanksgiving group could imagine. As the central heat is turned up to keep the chill off the house, we cook on our electric stoves and ovens. We turn on the running water to rinse our dirty dishes before we turn on the electricity to operate our dishwasher. We reach for the telephone to speak to loved ones that were not able to be with us. Then we get in our automobiles to drive to our different destinations – in time for different ones to get home to see their favorite football games.

Granted, we don't know how this first group of thanksgivers would have acted with all of the modern conveniences. I choose to believe they were much more focused on the true spirit of giving thanks and would not have been distracted as we have been.

I heard a friend on the phone with his sister last night, and they were having quite a heated argument about whether their family would fix a traditional dinner at home or all go sit together at a restaurant. I can see pros and cons for both sides of the argument, but the hurt and anger that I could hear from one side of the conversation made me very sad. My friend finally came back into the room where I was, and he was so disgusted that he had decided he would skip Thanksgiving with his family. After I calmed him down a little, I asked him to tell me again the name of the holiday coming up. Sheepishly, he told me. His grandmother is older and not in excellent health; and even though we do not know from one minute to the next if any of us will be here next year, I used her as an example. I told him that – no matter if I had Thanksgiving in a shack or the grandest restaurant in the world – my mom and my loved ones, who have gone on to the real Thanksgiving Feast, would not be there to share their love, corny jokes, and tales of their childhood with me. I think I made my point. He shed a few tears.

I always had a soft spot in my heart for MARTHA, the sister in the Bible who rushed around getting a meal ready for Jesus and all those at her home. I used to think: "Well, if not for Martha, there would have been no meal." However, it was MARY that CHRIST commended because she felt it more important to spend time with HIM while she could. As I grow older, I appreciate more and more what JESUS was saying. If I had my life to live over, I would spend more quality time listening and enjoying the people over the years who have meant so much to me and less time being sure we had such a bountiful meal that we were all miserable when we finished. Food is fuel for our bodies and nothing more, but time well spent with friends and loved ones enrich our total life experience.

In the movie "Places in the Heart," many cruel, racial, and unintentional mistakes were made. It was a sad movie, but the last scene made a terrific impact on me. I equated it with what I think HEAVEN will be like. At the end of the movie, they are in church singing a hymn and all the people who were hurt or killed in the movie – both black and white – were all in the pew singing together. They all seemed happy, loving, and at peace.

This Thanksgiving as my ninety-three-year-old father says the blessing, I will mentally be seeing all of my loved ones and friends who are absent in body but very much present in spirit. Most of all, I will be especially sensitive to the family and friends I still have and my BLESSINGS TOO NUMEROUS TO MENTION.

PICTURES OF THE MIND

I have always been a great one for taking photographs of every important occasion. As I grow older, I realize that we enjoy the photos for a few days after we take them and then they are stored away and hardly ever looked at again.

The older I get, the more I find the pictures that are truly captured are the vivid ones we take with the "camera" in our minds. These pictures never fade or discolor, and we can recall them at a moment's notice.

The Virgin Mary understood this principle when JESUS was born, when the WISE MEN came, and when JESUS was crucified before her very eyes. I know now what it means when the BIBLE says, "Mary kept these things and pondered them in her heart." According to Webster, PONDER means "to think deeply about" or "to contemplate, to reflect, and absorb." Since I have learned this method of remembering, I am not so adamant about the physical photograph because I realize that the really important things are recorded with the mental camera that is always in focus with vibrant color and a sharpness not known to man.

We record both pleasant experiences and disasters and can pull them up anytime. Those of my generation all remember where we were when World War II ended, the day FDR died, the day President Kennedy was shot, and the day CHALLENGER blew up. We can always remember the picture of the fireman carrying the dead child out of the wreckage of the Oklahoma federal building bombing and the TV coverage of these disasters. Sometimes there are mental pictures we wish we could erase, but they remain in the mind's camera.

We remember good things also. We all remember happy family occasions: the day we were married, the day each of our children were born, the day our children were married, and when they gave us grandchildren. I want to tell you about a new photo that was captured in my mind yesterday.

My grandson, Zach, now nine years old, had gone down the church aisle to give his heart to JESUS a couple of years ago. Since we sometimes forget that JESUS says we must all become as little children, we decided to wait on his baptism until we felt sure he knew what he was doing. He has been an inspiration to us all. Anytime he has trouble, he drops to his knees immediately and talks to JESUS about it. I am ashamed to admit that he has, on more than one occasion, reminded me that I can do the same thing. He is also the one who instantly falls to his knees when the pastor prays in church.

My son had a co-worker in Indiana who became a very dear friend. He was going to the seminary and has for the last few years been an ordained minister preaching GOD'S WORD. A couple of years ago, he began to experience symptoms of an illness that even Mayo Clinic and others were unable to identify. He has steadily gone down hill. He has no feeling in his hands or legs, and he has wasted away until he brings to mind skin stretched over a skeleton. He is in a wheelchair and is bedridden much of the time. The only thing that this unnamed malady has NOT been unable to deteriorate is his belief in GOD and his determination to serve and praise GOD with his dying breath.

Yesterday his mother and his family had a reunion at a state park, knowing this would be the last one he would attend. We are in the catering business and furnished the food they requested. We were all shocked at the way he looked. He was in his wheelchair and had his oxygen on. I have a breathing problem myself; and his first concern was for me, saying he would share his oxygen with me if I needed it. He was upbeat and was interested in everyone who attended.

After the meal, his large, strapping sons-in-law carried him down a large number of steps to get him in the lake to baptize my grandson. He requested that my son participate in this occasion because he wanted Zach to know he had a HEAVENLY FATHER who he could go to with his problems; but he also had an EARTHLY FATHER that would be available anytime he needed him.

Probably forty or so family members were there to witness the baptism. Since we were in a public lake, there were many grown-ups and children swimming and playing close by. Both the grown-ups and the children stopped their play and were very quiet. They joined in the applause when Zach came up out of the water. GOD works in mysterious ways, and we may never know how many hearts GOD spoke to that day. I don't think there was a dry eye in the crowd.

It was a grueling task for him and his family carrying him – but, oh, what an object lesson in faith and service. He had suffered so much that it would have been easy for him to say, "I can't do it." However, because of his love of GOD and my son, he used strength that could have been supplied only from above to accomplish this task. His sister said, with tears in her eyes, "I hope one day Zach will realize that he was the last one my brother ever baptized."

After he got back to the beach house, he had to go straight to bed because of his fatigue. He gave Zach a baptismal certificate which his sister filled out and he signed. The sacrifice GOD'S servant made that day was beautiful and impacted each of us involved.

As each of us leaned down to say what was almost inevitably our last "good-bye," we cried. It was hard. We assured him of our love and prayers, and he told us he would see us again in a better place. Secretly, we all hoped that God would see fit to take him out of this world and give him that new and "incorruptible body" we are promised. I think it is safe to say that none of us will need a photograph to remember this occasion. Although broken in body, GOD'S SERVANT had the spiritual strength to explain to a nine-year-old boy and his dad about their spiritual relationship to each other and GOD and then baptize my grandson.

I know, for myself, I will PONDER this experience the rest of my life. Thank You, DEAR FATHER, for this beautiful picture of a Spirit-filled life that can never be erased. Our friend died on December 13, 1999. He spent Christmas last year with the "CHRIST CHILD."

STRETCHING IS ESSENTIAL

I am a member of a twelve-step program, and the road is definitely not a smooth one. We will encounter "potholes" and dark, forbidding curves where there is only enough light to stay on the road. The AA Big Book invites newcomers to TRUDGE with them the Happy Road of destiny.

TRUDGING is defined as a laborious, tedious, weary walk. I think this clearly defines what we may expect on this road. It has always seemed a contradiction in terms to use TRUDGE and HAPPY in the same sentence when describing this walk; but the longer I strive for recovery, the more I realize they are not contradictions but two necessary elements to accomplish GOD'S GOAL in our lives.

I always wanted to avoid the TRUDGING part and SKIP rapidly to the HAPPY part. Only recently have I learned that one is absolutely essential to achieve the other. However, I am now at a point where I realize they can and do take place simultaneously.

We can never achieve SPIRITUALITY (a close, working, personal relationship with GOD) without pain and suffering. The Bible tells us we should rejoice in tribulation because it is proof that GOD is working in our lives. None of us like suffering and pain, and we do all we can to avoid them. However, if we look back over our lives, we realize these painful periods in our lives were the times we most often sought GOD'S INTERVENTION, resulting in periods of spiritual growth. This growth was brought about by desperation and total dependence on GOD.

When everything in our lives is going well, we have this illusion that we are in control. This is never true. We lull ourselves into this illusion, and we believe it so strongly that we forget how much we need GOD. Only in times of despair and helpless hopelessness do we grasp reality and know that our source for anything we have or enjoy is entirely dependent on our Heavenly Father.

With each such episode, we learn. When we revert to selective amnesia and we forget, another learning experience will be put in our path. GOD keeps putting the same lessons in our path until we learn them.

We know we will never be perfect in this life, but we should be striving for spiritual perfection. Only GOD can propel us toward that goal.

One day when we were having an especially hard time financially, I reminded my husband that this was another LEARNING EXPERIENCE. He laughed and said, "I have learned about all I want to learn for now." We all feel this way from time to time; but if we stay in a spirit of gratitude, we are able to TRUDGE and be HAPPY at the same time.

A dear friend of mine reminded me the other day about making a gratitude list. We should not list first all of the temporal things we have – such as jobs, family, friends, etc. – because any of these can be changed in the twinkling of an eye. Friends and family may die; jobs may be lost; homes may burn down; and finances may collapse. We should first list the spiritual blessings we have that will never change – such as GOD'S ETERNAL PRESENCE with us, HIS UNCONDITIONAL LOVE, HIS FORGIVENESS, and the fact that HE knows all about us and loves us anyway.

When our focus becomes God-centered, we are not buffeted so much back and forth in the storms of life. GOD did not promise there would be no storms, but He did promise HIS PEACE and PROTECTION while the storms are raging.

Our hearts are stretched each time GOD brings us victoriously to the other side of a painful experience. This process enables us to be more useful, tolerant, and loving of those around us that GOD would have us help. As any athlete will tell you, stretching is boring, painful, and ABSOLUTELY necessary to win or even finish a race. TRUDGING is necessary to stretch our hearts and experience. My son says, "Pain stretches the heart, so we will have room for all the joy!" Therefore, the road of destiny that we TRUDGE can also – at the same time – be HAPPY because of the prize we know is waiting at the end of the road.

HIS FACE / MAKE PEACE EVERY DAY

*W*hen I make a gratitude list, I sometimes forget some very important things. While talking with a friend of mine today, I remarked that I had been house bound for several weeks. She asked, "How do you stand it? I stay inside for two days, and I am suicidal!"

As I pondered her question, I realized something very important. I said, "I once felt the same way; but now I like myself more than I once did, and I know I am not really alone. God is with me, and we talk all day long. I don't stay on my knees all day; but I fellowship with Him, and He leads me into little projects to keep me entertained."

Years ago, I would do anything to keep from being alone. The minute I walked in the house, the TV, the radio, and the telephone were all utilized to keep from facing my insecurities and myself. It was not rapists or burglars I feared; it was having time to think about all of my shortcomings and me.

God has taken away that self-loathing and perfectionist side of me and replaced it with a softer, more forgiving side that loves me as I am – "warts and all." This side is not judgmental or mean, and it has made a happier existence for me – as well as those around me.

The Bible says, "Love thy neighbor as thyself." Since I now love myself, I can more easily love my neighbor. The poet said, "To thine own self be true, and thou canst be false to any man." Only when we love ourselves can we truly love others.

To love myself, I must keep my eyes off my imperfections and on His Perfect Face. To have His peace, I must seek it on a daily basis.

HIS FACE

On every side there is worry and care.
When I'm on my own, it seems too much to bear.
I worry and worry about my heavy load.
Everyone that I love seems on the wrong road.

I'm blind, but I struggle to keep them in place.
Then I turn to You and see Your sweet face.
A voice says, "Don't worry and try to be Me.
I'm in control! You never can be."

When I look up into HIS FACE, I peer –
The chaos around me does not disappear;
But it's out of my sight and my burden gets light
Because MY FATHER lifts me out of my night.

Freedom returns! I'm not in control.
In HIS LOVING ARMS, HE nurtures my soul.
Thanks once again, Father, for helping me see
There is only one GOD and it's surely not me!

MAKE PEACE EVERY DAY

Dear God, I have these problems
That seem so large to me.
They've rearranged my whole life.
From their grip, I can't get free.

My pride and independence
Have always had control,
But these problems that enslave me
Have reversed my every role.

I always was the caretaker
To meet the other's need.
I thought I had the answers –
If my advice they all would heed.

Now YOU have quite a different role
YOU feel that I should learn –
If I'm to be YOUR VESSEL,
My serenity to earn.

Now I have to ask for help
To get the things I need.
Many days I fail at this;
But on some days, I succeed.

The problems are long-term ones;
They're most likely here to stay.
Only I can make the choice, dear LORD,
How to handle them each day.

Each morning I get on my knees
And pray that I'll be willing.
Some days I can; some days I can't –
Depending if my life You're filling.

If I "boot out" self-pity
And get out of the way,
YOU come in and all goes well.
It's my choice how long YOU'LL stay!

I wish that once would settle things,
Granting peace without delay;
But I am finding more and more
We must seek peace every day.

MY DADDY

*M*y dad is ninety-four years young and is a "rock" and a blessing in the lives of all his friends and family. He has always been a strong man who could do almost anything to which he put his mind. He is a wonderful Christian with very strong principles. Right and wrong never wavered for him. Everyone always knew where he stood because he told them in no uncertain terms. No matter how much he disagreed with those around him, he still loved them just as much and let them know it (even Republicans).

My dad has never been a "touchy, feely" sort of man because he wasn't raised that way. Recently, my younger son hugged him; and my dad said, "I don't know about this business of men hugging." Being politically correct was the least of his worries. It has always been hard for him to say "I love you" in words. When I am on the phone and say "I love you," he always answers back: "Same to you." Since my mother has been gone, he has managed to say it on rare occasions; and we all treasure the times he actually says the words. This does not mean, however, that there is ever any doubt in our minds that he loves us and will be there any time we need him.

When he was sixty years old, he fell and broke his hip. He worked at the Naval Air Station as a metal smith. After his accident, he could not stand all day on those concrete floors; so he just chose to retire. Many people felt this was a big mistake. They thought he would sit down and give up. Oh contraire! He worked harder and accomplished more after his retirement than most people do in their whole lifetime.

He was treasurer of First Baptist Milton for thirty-three years. He served as a school trustee in the era of segregation. I can remember the principal of the all-black high school coming and talking to him late at night about how he could help him. He served on the Milton City Council for three terms (one he was elected to and others when he was requested to serve out someone else's term). He taught a teen-aged boys Sunday school class. He took me and my other four sidekicks all over to football games, band festivals, and any place else we needed or wanted to go. Both of my brothers played football for Milton High, and he was always there to watch.

Daddy has never been one to praise you to your face. I remember one time I came home with a report card with all A's – except for one B; and he said, "Why did you make a B?" However, he surely tooted your horn behind your back. One time when my children were young, he told me, "If you can get them grown without them stealing, you'll be doing okay." I thought at the time that he surely did not expect much of his children. Now that mine are grown, I know what he meant.

When my oldest son was about two years old, we lived in Montgomery, Alabama. When we came for a visit and went to church, he would cry if we left him in the nursery alone. Old, tough Gran Gran couldn't stand it; so he would stay with him. He was so good with the kids that the nursery ladies asked him to please keep helping them. He laughs and says, "I went to stay with David one Sunday and ended up staying twenty-two years." He could quiet children who would not respond to anyone else.

His grandchildren are very fortunate to have such a wonderful person in their lives. They all think Gran Gran can do anything. If there was an appliance or anything he couldn't fix, you might as well throw it away.

He did not give his grandchildren a lot of money or things. He gave the most important things – his time and himself. They always knew he was special – even though they picked on him and played tricks, but he gave them as good as he got. He taught his two grandsons to play golf, and he carried them and their friends (also golfers) to tournaments all over. They called themselves "RUBE'S RAIDERS," and they are still all excited to see him after twenty-five or more years have passed.

It turned out that his granddaughter Sharon played golf also, but he never took her along (he didn't know exactly what to do with girls). As fate would have it, Sharon was the one who went to the University of Alabama on a golf scholarship. I think some of the guys were embarrassed, but Gran Gran was proud.

Because I worked, my kids always spent most of the summer with Mother and Daddy. They were always at the country club during the day. My older son played golf, while his sister and younger brother preferred the pool. Russ and Gran Gran would take a two- or three-week trip in my daddy's Volkswagen camper, and they had a ball. Recently, Russ, who is now thirty-five, told me if he could relive any part of his life, it would be his trips with Gran Gran. On one trip, Russ was about twelve and was into collecting beer cans. Gran Gran said he had to stop and let Russ dig in every garbage can between Milton and Wyoming.

Not only is he a great friend, father, and grandfather; but he was also a good, faithful husband to my mother for sixty-five years. It took me a few years to realize that they made love at the top of their voices. The time to worry was when they were not arguing. He took wonderful care of my mother – after most would have had her in a nursing home. He could never have done it without Leah's help. He was determined that Mother was going to stay home as long as he could last. Many times after her mind was gone, we would be down visiting and we would want to go out to eat and bring her something back; but he was adamant that she dress, put on her makeup, and go too. He said, "If she doesn't get up and move, then she won't be able to; and then I can't take care of her, and that is not going to happen."

He kept her moving, going places, and treating her like his "beloved wife" as long as she lived. It was certainly an object lesson to us all – as well as others – of what "in sickness and in health" means in the wedding vows.

Honesty is a given as far as my daddy is concerned. You did not need a written contract with him because a handshake or his word was just as binding to him. I'm sure that is one reason he took care of Mother to the end. He had taken vows and made a contract with her, and it would never run out as far as he was concerned.

When the headstones were set at the cemetery after my mother died, he only asked for one thing, and that was a set of wedding rings carved between their two headstones. He said, "I guess after sixty-five years we deserve that."

He never did the little things that most people just take for granted or think of as "little, white lies." He always reported every little bit of "jury duty" money, cash someone paid him for a birdhouse he built, or money for working on the polls. My brother Richard, who has been a CPA for many years, always does his income tax for him; and Daddy is frantic and can't relax until he knows it is done and mailed.

We all have a good laugh when we remember the time he accidentally passed a stopped school bus and promptly came home to report it. They told him not to worry about it. I'm fairly sure his children and grandchildren are not quite that honest.

One of the most wonderful aspects of my daddy's life is his prayer life. Many times I have walked in on his prayer time, and I heard how he prays for each of us. I have seen him on his knees by my mother's hospital bed. At home, I have seen him on his knees, praying for my father-in-law when he was dying with colon cancer. I am assured every day, just knowing I have his unconditional love and prayers. The greatest gift a father can give his child is to help him see what our "HEAVENLY FATHER" is like and to hold high a standard of living that proves he believes what he says.

For many years – every time I called home, Daddy would say "Hi" and hand the phone to Mother. She was usually the "middleman" who told me what Daddy thought and told him what I thought. In the past few years since she has been gone, we have learned to talk to each other. I could sit for hours and listen to him tell me about his growing-up years in Bagdad Florida. Even the sad depression stories help me understand why people in that era think as they do. He is a very intelligent man; and with a little more education and a lot more self-confidence, he could have been the kind of politician we need today.

One of the last few times I visited in Milton, Daddy said, "Do you want to go to the nursing home to see a distant cousin of ours?" I said, "No, not particularly" – to which he replied, "Well, get dressed. You're going anyway!" Even though I am sixty-four years old – when I walk in my daddy's house, I am five years old again. I got dressed and we went. Not only did he take me to see the person he mentioned, but he took me to see everyone in residence. I mostly stood around, while he talked to everyone. I guess he sensed that I was past ready to go, and he said something I will never forget. He said, "Gay, these are the forgotten people that no one wants or cares much about anymore. Someone needs to care about them because, but for the GRACE OF GOD, it could be us." To say I was put kindly in my place was the understatement of the decade. I usually think of myself as a caring and giving person, but that statement from someone his age really hit home.

He always prays for "the forgotten people." Sometimes caring for others decreases with age, but in his case I think it has increased.

As I get older, I find myself saying, "I'm too old to do that anymore." I don't believe my daddy ever even considers such a thing. Even as his health is failing, I can't keep up with him. Once when I was scolding him about overdoing, he told me rather sternly, "My daddy died with a heart attack. My mother died with a heart attack. My brothers and sister died with a heart attack. Most likely, I will too; but I ain't going to be sitting around waiting for it."

He wasn't!

EMMALEIGH

J could not finish this book without telling you about my precious, little great-granddaughter. She is six now and the light of my life. Like so many teenagers, her mom was misled when she was sixteen. Emmaleigh was born when her mother was seventeen over the protest of everyone, including the doctor. My granddaughter said, "All my life, my mom and my grammy have drilled in my head that if you get pregnant, you HAVE the baby!" Because Emmaleigh's mom was adopted, she knew that from the day we got her when she was four pounds, fifteen inches long, and four days old that we always spoke of "our miracle" from God and that she was very loved.

My granddaughter has had a hard time, but she has always done the best she knew how to be a good mother. She was luckier than most girls in her situation because she had a great deal of family support.

Many might say her pregnancy was a big mistake. That absolutely was not the case. God sent Emmaleigh for us to love – just like her mom was sent.

Emmaleigh has long blond hair (which she has cut herself on several occasions); beautiful, blue trusting eyes; and a little attitude that is beyond description (such as when we ask her why she hit a child at school, she replied without hesitation, "Because he needed hitting!") She can always give you a plausible explanation for anything she does. She used to love to get a pen or marker when the grownups weren't looking and draw murals on freshly painted walls or on herself. She got in trouble so many times that if she found a pen or marker she would bring it to me and say, "You better take this." It never crossed her mind to just not do it. I have the same problem myself sometimes.

She walks around in those play high heels (the ones with the back out) all day some days. I haven't been able to do that in years. Her older cousin taught her how to sit with her legs crossed like a young lady; so if she is writing on a pad, she looks like a miniature secretary to F. Lee Bailey.

She loves to watch me put on makeup; and because I have Rosacea, sometimes I have to start with this green makeup to help hide the red. As I was doing this one day, as matter of factly as possible, she said, "Grammy, why are you putting that 'Grinch' makeup on you?" Another day as she was watching, I was asked, "Grammy, is that 'Oil of ALADDIN' you are putting on your face?"

She sits by me in church every Sunday, and last Sunday she asked me how to spell my name. When I showed her how, she copied it and drew a red heart by it. Only when she has children and grandchildren will she know how precious that was.

We are building a new sanctuary. The thirty-foot cross that will be on top was placed on tables behind the present church, and everyone was asked to sign it before it was overlaid. I took Emmaleigh to sign it, and she was very impressed. Most people signed in black, but her little name was signed in purple.

My husband Rich, who passed away in 2000, thought Emmaleigh was the grandest thing ever. He called her his "angel," and I like to believe he saw her write her precious name there. I hope when she gets older, she will understand that as a family we pray for her to be sure she has her name written in "The Lamb's Book of Life."

I thank God that He can see the "Big Picture" and He always gives us what we need – no matter what we think we want. God is good!

FEAR

*A*s GOD'S CHILDREN, we have many emotions to deal with from day to day. They run the gambit from love to hate, anger to understanding, wishing one's fellowman well to being envious and selfish. We vacillate between self-pity and an attitude of gratitude which we all have – if we really take stock of our lives and see, hear, and experience all of the wonders God has provided for us. Many things are given to us freely, and we never even recognize how important they are or where they come from.

In my own life, I have found that the emotion I have the most trouble with is this little word "FEAR." It can appear almost from out of nowhere; and before we even realize this is the emotion that is our problem, we may be completely paralyzed and unable to function like intelligent human beings. It distorts our thinking and causes us to act in ways that hurt us and everyone around us.

As we grow spiritually, we are ashamed to admit our fear to ourselves – and certainly to others. We feel if we had enough faith, fear could not attack us; so we try to keep our fears inside and deal with them alone. Actually, quite the reverse is true. Fear is an emotion that even the most spiritual of people deal with from time to time.

Fear is a deep-seated defect, and I am powerless to deal with it on my own. Only as I admit my powerlessness and ask God to take my fear away am I relieved of that heavy, anxious, all-engulfing feeling that makes it impossible for me to enjoy life as God intends His children to do.

Now when I begin to berate myself for feeling fear, which is indigenous to all humanity, I am reminded that in human form even JESUS sweated drops of blood because of His fear of being separated from His Father. Just as fear is occasionally inevitable in all of our lives; so is the removal of that fear – if we ask God to take it away and are willing to be patient and remember God has His own TIMETABLE.

FEAR

Fear is such a little word,
An evil and corroding thread.
It runs around inside my heart
And fills my life with dread.

I feel so very guilty
When this defect enters in.
It seems that I am paralyzed.
I don't know where I should begin.

I'm ashamed to let others know
This anxiety I feel.
I think if I ignore it
These feelings won't be real.

I forget that I am human
When these feelings start to flood.
I forget that even JESUS CHRIST
In the garden sweated blood.

So why should I be so surprised.
Fear is normal – that is true;
But when I share my feelings,
It helps both me and you.

When I admit I'm powerless
And give my fear away,
Then God steps in and gets results
When I get out of HIS WAY.

His eye is on the sparrow.
Just watch and you will see.
"If HIS EYE is on the sparrow,
Then I know HE watches me!"

HEY! PRETTY LADY

*A*s I was doing my devotional this morning, one of the comments in one of the books I was reading reminded me that our real purpose in this life is not fame or the amassing of great wealth. Wealth is not, in itself, a bad thing; but if we are so obsessed in the pursuit of it that we do not have time for anything or anyone else, then that obsession becomes our GOD. When we are in the throws of this obsession, we tend to have our priorities in the wrong order. According to the Bible, our real vocation in this life is to do GOD'S WILL and serve our fellowman.

For many years, I felt that everyone's happiness was my responsibility. If the ones I loved were having a hard time, I felt it was my job to "fix it." I stayed "strung out" most of the time because it was an impossible task and was certainly not the role GOD had assigned me. Physically, emotionally, and spiritually, I was always on empty because I was so "full" of myself trying to achieve the impossible in a position that only GOD can fill.

Because it takes me so long to learn anything of a spiritual nature, GOD puts large spiritual signs on my road map. One of these large signs was my husband. He was perhaps the most gentle, loving, and kind man I had ever known and certainly one of the most wonderful examples of what a Christian should be that GOD ever put on this earth.

Now by saying this, I do not mean he was perfect. He had some faults because he was human; but if you were to follow him around for a day or two or listen to him talk on the telephone, you would get a real education in the "little" things that mean so much.

It is a family joke – although we all admired him more than most anyone we knew – how he spoke to everyone and tried to make them feel good. He could not help it! It was just part of his nature.

Sometimes when we were in a department or grocery store or in a restaurant and he saw someone who looked as if he had been on his feet for hours and had a pained and weary expression on his face, without even thinking Rich would go into action.

He learned early on that people like to hear their name. He immediately looked for a name tag; so if at all possible, he could call them by name. With the ladies and young girls, he always said, "Hey, pretty lady" – followed by: "Anyone named Sally (or Jean, etc. – whatever the name might be) has to be okay." With men his line was: "Hey, young fellow"; and with the young boys, it was: "Hey, big guy" (remembering that teenage boys don't especially want to be reminded they are young – just like the old ones like being called young.)

He loved children – and especially babies. He never saw a young mother or dad in a store or most anywhere that he did not stop to play with the baby and tell the parents how beautiful their child was. All parents like to feel their child is special and are always happy when someone else recognizes their child as exceptional and comments on it. They always walked away with their shoulders back and a smile on their face. You could tell visibly they were refreshed.

Was he always truthful? I THINK NOT! Some of the women he called "Pretty Lady" would have had to slip up on a glass of water to get a drink. Some of the men he called "Young Fellow" were older than dirt. Some of the "Big Guys" were scrawny, pimply-faced, little guys who didn't weigh over ninety pounds soaking wet and were only five feet tall. Sometimes the babies he said were so beautiful looked somewhat like WINSTON CHURCHILL in the face. But does that really matter?

Just like GOD and I are on different time schedules, so were my husband and I. I have a tendency to rush from place to place without really seeing things and people around me. I usually go in one place with one goal on my agenda. I want to fulfill that goal and "hit the bricks."

My husband, however, seemed to dawdle everywhere he went. Most of the time, it was an infuriating inconvenience to me. If I was really in a "fit" spiritual condition, I could see the method in his madness; so I relaxed and watched him work.

Rich was the most unselfish man I knew; but deep down, I knew he must be getting something from these actions for himself. I think it was the same feeling I got when I returned the twenty to a cashier who thought she gave me a ten. It made ME feel good. He knew for the two or three minutes he took to compliment these people, they received a few minutes of feeling good about themselves. That was his reward!

Unfortunately, times are changing – as I had to remind him when he stopped to talk to a child in the grocery store or wherever. Parents nowadays are nervous because of all the child snatching and meanness that goes on, and they might misunderstand that he just loved children. It is a sad commentary on our society that our civilization has come to this sorry state, but facts are facts. Kids nowadays receive such mixed messages that they don't know what to do. They are told not to talk to strangers; and then in the next instant, they are told to talk to someone they don't know and tell them their name. No wonder they are confused! I encouraged Rich not to do it when he was alone because that looked even more suspicious. He was, however, incorrigible; and I'm sure he continued to do it – in spite of my warnings.

I try to remember to be kind to everyone, but I am not as diligent as he was. Most of the time, I forget that the BIBLE says, "Be kind to one another because you may be entertaining ANGELS unawares." I get so wrapped up in the temporal things that it escapes me that only spiritual things have any true or lasting effect.

How often do we pass up JESUS disguised as a weary waitress, a frustrated young parent, a lonely shut-in, or very often members of our own family? A warm smile and friendly greeting is such a little thing. We often forget that such a simple act might be the bright spot in someone's day. If we are walking a spiritual walk, it is a natural phenomenon that GOD'S LOVE overflows into the lives of others. We do not have to worry about running out of good things because GOD never leaves us "empty" – except when we are too "full" of ourselves.

My husband worked hard, and he was very busy; but he was never too tired or too self-absorbed to care about his fellowman. When he died, I am convinced GOD said to him, "Well done, thou good and faithful servant." Then St. Peter opened the gates and shouted, "Hey, here comes the 'Pretty Lady Man'!"

DEAR MISS AMERICA

*O*n March 4, 2003, I became the proud grandmother of Lauren Grace Poe. She weighed in at eight pounds and seven ounces and was twenty-two and one-fourth inches long. Her father Russ is my youngest son. Since she is my baby's baby, she is very special.

Her dad is thirty-eight years old and, therefore, somewhat older than most of his friends when they first became parents. He is notorious for getting all little kids he knows all wired and running around like wild Indians. Then he decides he is ready to quit playing, leaving both the children and their parents frustrated and in somewhat of a bad mood. When the kids did not stop when he did, Russ suggested that their bad behavior was the result of the "complete lack of home training."

I told him recently I have contracted for Phillips Arena in downtown Atlanta (it is completely sold out by the way) to see how he handles parenting. He was a "holy terror" when he was young and still has a bowl of "Purina BRAT CHOW" for breakfast occasionally. His wife Kelly is a beautiful woman – both inside and out; and because I love her so much, I would never want her to go through rearing a child like her husband.

The following is a letter I wrote to Lauren while I was waiting and praying for her to be born. Actually, she is a very blessed little girl to have parents who love her so much.

Truthfully, I will feel very happy if she grows up and makes me nearly as proud of her as I always have been of her dad. I am praying that Kelly will have the strength to raise her children (both Lauren and Russ). Of course, being his mother, I think his sweet and childlike spirit is one of his most lovable qualities.

MARCH 4, 2003

Dear "Miss America,"

You don't know me yet. I am the one sitting in Georgia, biting my fingernails down to the nub and waiting to hear that you have been born. I jump every time the phone rings. I am your dad's mom, which makes me your "Grammy." I have loved you since I first heard you were coming into this world. I have prayed every day for you, your mom, and your dad. I have especially prayed each day for your health and that of your precious mom. Like everyone else, I can't wait to meet you. I can only imagine how precious you will be.

This world can be a very scary place sometimes. You are very fortunate that you are surrounded by such a network of people who love you. You will never have to lack for it. I thank GOD that you are being born into a family with a beautiful mom and a dad who will love you unconditionally with all their hearts. Some children are not so fortunate, and they soon find out about the scary world I am talking about at an early age.

You are such a beautiful gift from GOD. I pray we will all remember that you are only on loan to us. You are a sacred trust that GOD has given to us to love, cherish, and protect as long as HE sees fit to leave us together. Your job is to grow strong and straight, and ours is to point you to GOD and heaven from where you came.

I have been thinking about your "Poppy" not getting to see our new, little princess because I know how much he would have doted on you. Then I think that he has probably seen you and held you and knew that you were his "Star's" little girl. There is a myth that before a baby comes into the world they know everything; and just before they are born, GOD puts HIS FINGER over the top lip and says "SHOO," so they won't tell us. Maybe GOD let "Poppy" do that. I just feel that all the family members – on both sides that have gone on – know and love you.

It is hard to believe you can love anyone who you haven't met or even seen – as much as I already love you. You be sweet for your mom and dad because they are your best friends. GOD BLESS YOU, my darling. Welcome to this world and welcome to this family.

Love, Grammy

THE LITTLE GREEN LEAF

*A*s I had mentioned at the beginning of this endeavor, I wrote my (what I laughingly call) first poem at the age of four or five. I also remember how thrilled I was when I discovered the recessive gene from my Great-Great-Grandfather Jernigan was probably the reason I ever started writing poetry. It was a reminder of how God's cycle continues, and I feel it is very exciting.

God is always giving me little nudges and little gifts to make my life fuller. Many times it seems He uses these little gifts to prompt me along the path I should take.

Since I have begun this project, there have been many changes in my life. My health problems have gotten worse. Family relationships have changed. My husband and my parents have passed away. I have had many adjustments to make. Sometimes I forget that God will make these transitions less painful if I am willing to LET HIM!

A special gift God gave me – when I was trying to work through the grief process about my mom – was a reminder that GOD is in charge and His cycle is constant and perfect. This gift came in the following form: "Pris" called – very elated to tell me Casey, my then five-year-old granddaughter, had come in all excited to recite the poem she had written.

It is a very comforting feeling to know that GOD'S PLAN is perfect and infallible and as workable and sure today as it was before the beginning of time. I'm sure about the cycle because the song sung at my mother's funeral is one Casey sings around the house a lot. It says, "Because HE lives, I can face tomorrow." I personally believe in that promise. There is nothing my God and I can't face together.

THE LITTLE GREEN LEAF

One little green leaf on a tree
The wind blew round and round.
Then one little green leaf
Came tumbling down!

-- Casey Nicole Poe
Age 5

THE TRIP

*W*ell, here I am at the end of this fearsome road that GOD has urged me to follow. There have been many times when I wanted to quit because I doubted my faith, my commitment, and always my talent. After each such lapse, I would again feel that GOD wanted me to do this – and I would again take up the struggle.

As a child, I always wanted to make my earthly father proud. It has taken a long time for me to understand that. Even though I would like my efforts to make my HEAVENLY Father proud, I realize HE is the One who has furnished the inspiration, the strength, and yes, the courage to accomplish this task. I have to keep reminding myself that GOD is using me for some purpose; and if one thing in this book helps one person on their journey, then my effort will not be in vain.

Thank You, Dear Father, for being with me on every step of this wonderful journey. Forgive my side trips into weakness, faithlessness, and fear. Use this effort for Your GLORY.

THE TRIP

As I wander in Life's Forest,
I'm surrounded by great fears.
This journey seems so long and hard.
I shed so many tears.

From here, the way seems hopeless.
Cliffs and thorns align the way.
The darkness that surrounds me
Makes me stumble, and I stray.

The way is rough and rocky –
Little light that can be found.
Bruised and battered, I give up –
A sobbing child upon the ground.

In my despair, I hear a voice.
It's small and still and quiet.
It says, "My child, just hold MY HAND;
And things will be alright."

I recognize this still, small voice.
It's tried to speak before;
But if I feel that I'm in charge
When "IT" speaks, I close the door.

"Can I be sure You know the way
And You won't let me slip?"
"Not only will I walk with you.
It was 'I' who planned the trip!"

INDEX